Concept

Capitalism

A Social Audit

Peter Saunders

Open University Press
Buckingham

Open University Press
Celtic Court
22 Ballmoor
Buckingham
MK18 1XW

First published 1995

A catalogue record of this book is available from the British Library

ISBN 0-335-19141-X (pb)   0-335-19142-8 (hb)

Typeset by Type Study, Scarborough
Printed in Great Britain by J. W. Arrowsmith Ltd, Bristol

Contents

Preface   vii

1   The Growth Machine   1

2   Capitalism and the Poor Countries   29

3   Capitalism and the Environment   52

4   Capitalism and Human Happiness   77

5   The Future of Capitalism   102

Notes   121

Index   134

Preface

This book is an attempt to develop a social audit of contemporary capitalism and the path on which it is taking us.

For much of the twentieth century, the future of capitalism was in serious doubt. This is no longer the case, for the challenge from socialism has collapsed. Throughout the world wherever it has been tried, socialism has failed and is now rapidly being abandoned. Capitalism is poised to become a truly global phenomenon.

A book about capitalism today, therefore, needs to look forward and to identify the major issues which are likely to preoccupy us in the world which is emerging out of the rubble of the Berlin Wall. These issues no longer have to do with whether capitalism can survive – it can, and almost certainly will – but rather with the implications of its successful extension throughout the world.

There are, I believe, three major questions which arise today from the success of capitalism on a global scale, and in their different ways they all concern the nature of modern capitalism as an economic 'growth machine'. One is the question of whether the poorer countries of sub-Saharan Africa, Central and South America, southern Asia and China, and southern and eastern Europe can hope to 'catch up' with the advanced capitalist nations of North America, western Europe and Japan. Can capitalism revolutionize the living standards of the remaining 80 per cent of the world in the way that it has done for the rich 20 per cent? If it can, there is then the second question of whether the world can survive such a massive expansion of industrial output. Precisely because capitalism is so successful in harnessing nature to raise output, it seems to threaten the delicate ecological balance of the planet, and the growing force of green ideas in western nations reflects a widespread concern that we may be nearing the precipice of irreversible environmental catastrophe. Finally, there is the biggest and most significant question of all, for if and when capitalism has raised the population of the world from poverty and squalor and has successfully met the challenge of ecological extinction, there still remains the issue of whether humankind will be any better off than before. The rapid growth unleashed by capitalism has fundamentally changed the way we live, but are we any happier as a result?

These three questions are addressed in the three core chapters of this book. Chapter 2 considers the problems of development in the Third World; Chapter 3 is concerned with the issue of environmental survival; and Chapter 4 addresses the question of whether capitalism is ultimately compatible with the conditions required for human happiness. Before that I have outlined (in Chapter 1) why it is that capitalism has proved so successful in promoting technological change and economic growth, and how this revolutionary system of social and economic organization came into being in the first place. The book is then rounded off (in Chapter 5) with a brief consideration of the future of capitalism in a world where the socialist alternative has collapsed, but where new divisions and new challenges may now be emerging.

The book has benefited from the critical comments of friends and colleagues on earlier drafts of various chapters, and I should like to thank in particular David Harrison, Julie Koch and Luke Martell for their helpful advice and suggestions. Since all three remain sceptical with regard to many of the arguments developed in the book, I should add that the final responsibility for what follows remains mine alone.

The Growth Machine

In 1851, the British government invited the world to a 'Great Exhibition' of industrial products and machinery, held in London's Hyde Park in a purpose-built 'palace' of steel and glass. The Crystal Palace exhibition was a celebration of the new industrial age and of Britain's undisputed primacy among the emerging industrial nations. But it could also be seen as a celebration of the Victorian ideals of progress, enlightenment and modernity, of the conquest of nature by machines, and of the victory of a new social order in Europe. The fact that this extraordinary palace had been built to house machines and commodities rather than courtiers and gilded baubles vividly symbolized the transition from an old era based on the power of gods and kings to a new one based on the power of steam engines and entrepreneurs.[1] The Crystal Palace exhibition was the first great party to celebrate the emergence of a new social and economic system which was destined to revolutionize life on this planet – the system we know today as capitalism.

The *Oxford English Dictionary* traces the first reference to the word 'capitalism' in the writings of William Makepeace Thackeray in 1854, three years after the Great Exhibition and at least 15 years before capitalism's best-known critic, Karl Marx, began to use the term.[2] But capitalism did not begin in the mid-nineteenth century. It pre-dates the industrial revolution, for there were commercial capitalists long before there were factory owners, and there was widespread wage labour long before there was an industrial workforce.

Modern capitalism has its roots in trade, roots which lie deep in the soil of European history. As far back as the eleventh century, when the waves of Norman, Saracen and Magyar invasions in Europe gave way to a period of relative peacefulness, merchants began to develop commercial trade routes, open up new frontiers, and create a rudimentary system of international money and credit through the use of bills of exchange.[3] This expansion of trade led eventually to the growth of new centres of commerce and manufacturing in the Low Countries and in Italian cities such as Florence.

By the sixteenth century, when European nations began to extend their trade and their territorial claims westward into the Americas, and eastward into the Orient, commercial capitalism was well developed in northern Europe. By then, cities such as Antwerp and Amsterdam were functioning as major centres of commercial exchange, trading bullion from South America, timber from the Baltic, spices from the Far East and textiles from England. More importantly, capitalism had by then also begun to permeate industry and agriculture.

In the Middle Ages, industry and agriculture in much of Europe was organized around feudal principles which obliged serfs to work for the lords of the great estates on which they lived, while apprentices and journeymen in various trades were tied to guild masters in the towns. This system began to break down in England and the Netherlands from as early as the thirteenth century,[4] and by the sixteenth century it had in several parts of Europe effectively been replaced by a system of production based upon monetary payments. The expansion of trade was largely responsible for the erosion of feudalism, for it diffused a system of monetary exchange throughout Europe, gradually substituting cash payments for feudal duties and creating a market in land and in loans. Urban craftsmen and rural cottagers increasingly worked for wages from merchants who supplied them with their raw materials and who sold their finished products in markets which extended far beyond their immediate localities. While the feudal lords and princes managed in some parts of Europe to retain their power and social position well into the eighteenth and even the nineteenth centuries, the system which they represented had been eroded economically long before that.

By the time of the Great Exhibition, capitalism had thoroughly revolutionized the system of production in western Europe and was in the process of developing into a global system. The nineteenth century was the period when industrial capitalism consolidated its base in England and began to take over the world.

Today, as the twentieth century draws to a close, we are witnessing the final triumph of this capitalist world system. Not only the kings and princes of a previous age, but also the commissars and people's deputies of our own century, have found that political might is insufficient to resist the forces for change unleashed by the most dynamic economic system the world has ever witnessed. It took several centuries for capitalism to develop, but once established it has carried all before it.

What, then, are the key features of this system which has conquered the world? How does a capitalist system work? What is it about capitalism that generates such unprecedented economic growth and technological innovation? And how did a small corner of Europe stumble upon such an awesome system in the first place?

Private property, profit and the market

Capitalism is not the same in Scandinavia as in Hong Kong, not the same in Germany as in the United States, not the same in nineteenth-century England as in twenty-first-century Thailand. Capitalism takes different forms in different places at different times, but it is possible to identify certain key elements which together help to define it as a distinctive system. Three elements in particular appear fundamental in defining the basic features common to all capitalist systems.

The first is that capitalism entails *private ownership of property*, including those assets such as land, plant and raw materials which are employed in producing the goods and services on which the population depends. Private ownership of property entails three crucial rights which can be enforced over other people: the right of exclusive control and use of the property; the right exclusively to benefit from the exploitation of the property; and the right to dispose of the property as one sees fit.

One of the key differences between capitalist and socialist systems lies in the extent to which property rights are vested in private individuals or organizations. In the former Soviet Union, for example, ownership of resources such as land, buildings and machinery was vested primarily in public authorities, and private citizens had no exclusive rights of control, no way of identifying what was their share and differentiating it from what belonged to others, and no effective means of disposing of the property held nominally on their behalf by selling it, exchanging it, or bequeathing it to others. When a country moves from socialism to capitalism, a first step must always involve the re-creation of private property rights. From 1991 onwards, for example, the Russian government sought to privatize state property by allocating citizens individual shares which they could keep or sell as they chose, and within three years the private sector accounted for about half of the total economy. Similarly in China, where capitalism has been developing since the mid-1970s within the special economic zones (and to some extent outside them), an official stock exchange has now been established by the authorities to enable people to buy their own shares in enterprises, to profit from them, and to trade in them as they wish.[5]

Of course, most capitalist societies include elements of socialized property ownership. Western governments have often owned and run major industries including utilities such as gas and water and even huge car manufacturers such as Renault in France, although there has been a world-wide move in recent years to privatize many of these holdings.[6] Governments also often build and manage housing and provide other resources for their citizens such as insurance services and schooling. There are probably no examples in the world of a 'pure' capitalist system based entirely on private property. Rather, different societies are ranged on a continuum between those where most property is privately owned and those where property is vested mainly in the state. Capitalism does not, therefore, preclude a role for the state, but it does entail as little use as necessary of the political process.[7]

One important aspect of private property rights under capitalism is that they extend to individuals' ownership of their own bodies. Unlike slave systems (where individuals may be owned by others), feudal systems (where individuals are tied by lifelong obligations to others), and socialist systems (where labour can be directed by the communal authority and is not generally free to bargain over its level of remuneration), individuals in capitalist societies own their own bodies, and others only establish the right to use them through voluntary contract. Of course, as Marx argued, individuals who own no other resources may have little effective choice but to sell their brains or their muscles to an employer for a specified period of time each day,[8] but they are still free to determine their own choice of employer and to negotiate over the terms and conditions of their employment. The labour process under capitalism is therefore based upon the principle of contract rather than coercion, custom or duty. Forced labour (e.g. the indentured labour system in the British colonies in the nineteenth century, or conscripted 'national service' in many countries today) does exist under capitalism, but it is not the characteristic form of the labour process in capitalist societies.

The second key feature of capitalism is that economic activity is organized around the systematic and self-interested *pursuit of profit*. This, of course, is why private property ownership is fundamental to the operation of a capitalist system, for it is only when titles to property are held by private individuals and rights to benefit from the use of property are vested in owners that the 'profit motive' functions as the mainspring of economic activity. As Adam Smith recognized, capitalism is a system which mobilizes an appeal to individual self-interest as the mechanism for generating wealth.[9]

The pursuit of profit is not in itself a phenomenon unique to capitalism. For as long as there has been private property there have been individuals who have attempted, by coercion, craft or cunning, to augment their personal wealth.[10] Merchants, pirates, adventurers and Pharaohs have sought to expand their wealth ever since the beginnings of recorded history; and even under socialist regimes, those responsible for managing state resources have tried (and often succeeded) to use their position to their own personal advantage. What is distinctive about capitalism, however, is that everyday economic activity is structured around the methodical pursuit of ever renewed profit. Under capitalism, individuals produce goods or services, not for their own immediate consumption, nor in response to politically determined objectives set by slave-masters or economic planners, but in the hope and expectation that they will make profit.

This means that in capitalism, production is usually a means to an end rather than an end in itself. Goods and services will be produced where there is a reasonable expectation that profit can be made, and they will not be produced where there is no such expectation. Capitalism may therefore produce goods and services that many of us may deem 'unnecessary' or even harmful – it produces heroin as well as aspirin, pornography as well as art, tasteless trinkets and gaudy novelties as well as tractors, computers and dialysis machines. It also means that capitalism may not produce what many of us consider 'necessary'. Left alone, it will not produce food for people who cannot afford to buy it, schooling for people who cannot afford to pay for it, or housing for people who cannot afford to rent it. As Marx correctly argued, capitalism is interested, not in need but in profit, not in 'use values' but in 'exchange values'.

The subordination of production to calculations of likely profit means that capitalism tends to be characterized by a high degree of what Max Weber called 'formal rationality'.[11] For Weber, the epitome of this spirit of rationality is the system of double-entry bookkeeping, a system of accounting which can track every item of expenditure and match it to every source of revenue. But specialist accounting practices are not the only example of such meticulous and methodical calculation. Markets for new goods are exhaustively analysed by specialist research agencies and are then carefully cultivated through advertising. Retail sales are monitored at computerized supermarket check-outs which detect the slightest variations in patterns of consumer spending. The labour process is analysed for its efficiency by time-and-motion studies and is modelled on the latest theories of personnel management. Recruitment of labour may be delegated to specialist agencies and is based on formal criteria of qualifications, curricula vitae, aptitude tests and confidential testimonials. From beginning to end, the whole process of production is subjected to rational calculation in an attempt to make every stage, from the purchase of inputs to the sale of the finished product, as predictable and efficient as possible.

Modern corporate capitalism is more about improving profitability at the margin than it is about making a spectacular killing. Short-term speculation, high-risk gambles and opportunistic racketeering do, of course, occur in capitalist systems, and we shall see in Chapter 5 that modern American capitalism has become increasingly susceptible to corporate raiders and asset strippers concerned only to make a quick profit. Such behaviour can, however, only thrive on the margins of capitalist enterprise, just as vultures can only flourish if there are other animals around to provide the carcasses, and it tends to attract opprobrium as (in the words of a former British Conservative prime minister) the 'unacceptable face' of capitalism. Capitalism does entail risk but it does not generally sanction recklessness. It is inevitably influenced by short-term calculations of advantage, but this is normally tempered by the concern to accumulate profit to enable the entrepreneur to begin the next cycle of production with more resources than he or she had at the start of the previous one. The *leitmotiv* of modern capitalism is the parable of the three talents, not the story of the prodigal son.

The third key element of capitalism is that goods and services are exchanged on the basis of *market prices*. Modern capitalism is a money system in which the value of all goods and services can be expressed in a common value equivalent. Goods can be bartered in a capitalist system, but most exchange takes place for money rather than for other goods. It is the money system (initially in the form of precious metals, then in the form of coin and paper symbols, and later still in the form of ledger entries and electronic credit transfers) which has enabled capitalism to grow beyond the confines of individual localities and to expand the range of goods and services which are offered for sale, for money allows producers to create commodities without having first to find a consumer who wants them and who has a desirable commodity to exchange in return. Money, in other words, has enabled the separation of producers from the final consumers of their product, and this has expanded the scope of markets to a point where millions of transactions can now occur every hour in a way which would be impossible in a simple barter economy.

Raw materials and finished commodities are bought and sold for money on a (relatively) free market. However, just as property is rarely entirely in private ownership, so too markets are rarely completely free, for most governments regulate on issues such as the safety and desirability of products, many impose tariffs on goods from outside their own territory and tax flows of revenue, and some attempt from time to time to control prices. Nevertheless, a key feature of capitalism is that exchange occurs at a price which is principally determined by the point at which supply matches effective demand. This is true not only of exchange of goods, but also of exchange of other 'factors of production' including capital and labour. Money and workers both have a price which is expressed, respectively, in interest charges and wages, and these too are determined in a capitalist economy by the play of supply and demand.

Free markets, of course, are a source of uncertainty for capitalist producers, for they can never be sure that there are enough buyers out there willing and able to purchase their products at a price which will enable them to realize a profit. Various attempts are made to reduce this unpredictability, some of them legal (e.g. raw materials and currency can be bought and sold at a fixed price in advance on the futures markets), some not (industrial espionage, bribes and cartels are all examples of how companies may try to increase the predictability of the environment in which they operate). But for as long as markets remain competitive and relatively open, they can never be made wholly predictable – over 80 per cent of the new products launched on the American market each year fail.[12] Capitalism is inherently prone to lurch between gluts (caused by overproduction as companies invest heavily in response to favourable market signals) and shortages (as they all cut back together when they see goods piling up in warehouses and high street prices falling).

All of this contrasts with the system of production and exchange in non-capitalist economies. We have already seen that in feudal Europe there was effectively no market in land, for land could not be alienated, and only a very limited market in labour, for labour was tied to landed estates or to urban guilds. Even when a system of wage labour did emerge, minimum and maximum wages for different types of worker were often set by legislation. Trade in goods was also firmly regulated by governments, princes and guild masters who stipulated what could be bought and sold, by whom, at what price, and even how it should be transported and where the proceeds should be spent. Similarly, political and religious prohibitions on usury tightly restricted and regulated the market in money-lending.

The capitalist market system also contrasts vividly with socialist systems where most aspects of production and exchange were controlled through a comprehensive system of central state planning, and where movement of capital and labour into and out of the country was severely restricted. The reason for replacing the market mechanism by a system of state economic planning was, first, that it allowed governments to direct resources into producing what was needed and away from wasteful, damaging or frivolous investment (in most socialist countries, this meant that investment was heavily concentrated on building up industry and infrastructure and was directed away from production of consumer goods), and second, that the periodic crises of under- and overproduction in capitalist systems could in theory be avoided by coordinating the different parts of the economy around an agreed set of medium- and long-term targets. Socialist planning, in other words, was intended to overcome the 'anarchy of the market' by tying production to fixed and predictable targets rather than to fluctuating market prices.

We now know that this theory did not work in practice. The main reason why it did not work was that it proved impossible to coordinate all the different parts of a complex modern economy in the absence of market pricing.[13] As Mises, Hayek and other economists argued almost from the beginning of the Soviet experiment, the capitalist market system is first and foremost an information system.[14] If shortages occur in one sector of industry, or if consumers change their preferences, or if new technology makes existing manufacturing methods obsolete, all this shows up quickly in changing prices, and all other producers and consumers can adjust their own behaviour accordingly. In a centrally planned economy, there is no equivalent mechanism for transmitting this information. In the absence of price signals, producers have no effective means of monitoring their own activities in relation to those of other producers, and consumers have no effective means of transmitting changing preferences to those who are producing the goods. In such a system, coordination of the activities of millions of individuals becomes virtually impossible, and the famed shortages and inefficiencies of the Soviet and Chinese economies were the inevitable outcome.[15]

Capitalism defined

These three factors together – private ownership of property, production for profit, and a system of exchange based upon market prices – add up to a working definition of what capitalism is and how it differs from other systems such as feudalism and socialism. More specifically, we may define capitalism as a system in which individuals or combinations of individuals compete with each other to accumulate wealth by buying the rights to use land, labour and capital in order to produce goods or services with the intention of selling them in a market at a profit.

The growth machine

Capitalism is driven by the motive to accumulate profit. Given a system of private property and relatively free markets, the pursuit of profit brings entrepreneurs into competition with one another as each seeks to maximize profits by reducing the costs of inputs of land, labour and capital and by selling the finished product at the highest achievable price.

This competitive pursuit of profit means that capitalist enterprises are for ever looking to discover new markets, to develop new products and to exploit new technologies which reduce their costs of production. Each is looking to gain a competitive edge, and it is this that provides the impetus to change and innovation in capitalist systems.

Capitalism is a growth machine. The search for new markets has always driven it outwards, from the towns into the countryside, from England into Europe and the United States, from the centres of the nineteenth-century empires into the ex-colonial periphery of the 'Third World' in the twentieth century, and from the West into the former communist countries of the East. It was the impetus of trade that led to the revolutions in transportation and communications which first enabled social cohesion within nation-states and which then went on to transcend the boundaries between them. Steam power in the nineteenth century shrank the oceans and drove railways across the Rockies, over the Andes and through the Indian sub-continent. The internal combustion engine, the jet engine and electronic communications through cables and satellites have in the twentieth century shrunk nations and enabled instantaneous communication across continents. Capitalism has collapsed distance, overcome space and pulled the world together into an integrated (yet somewhat precarious and often dangerous) global system.

Capitalism triggered the industrial revolution, and the ever increasing and urgent search for new products and for new technologies which can raise productivity and lower costs has continued to revolutionize the way that we live ever since. This perpetual search by capitalist firms for a competitive advantage means that the rate of change is for ever speeding up. In just one hundred years we have witnessed the invention of the motor car, the provision of domestic electric lighting, the invention of television and other consumer durables such as washing machines and refrigerators, the development of air travel, the harnessing of nuclear power, the establishment of satellite communications, the beginnings of space travel, the invention of personal computers. Today we stand at the brink of a revolution in biotechnology and genetic engineering. The pace of development is breathtaking when we recall that five hundred years ago the only form of power machinery known to human beings was the water wheel.

Capitalist development has revolutionized the living standards which ordinary people now take for granted. In Britain, gross national income quadrupled between 1688 and 1801, quadrupled again between 1801 and 1871, and then quadrupled again between 1871 and 1924. Output per head of population increased fivefold in Britain between 1871 and 1989. The same pattern was then repeated in countries where capitalist industrialization began later. Since the 1870s, per capita output has risen ninefold in the USA, 11-fold in Germany, and by a factor of 25 in Japan.[16] These increases in national income and output have resulted in huge improvements in living standards. Real wages (i.e. the purchasing power of wages when allowing for inflation) have risen in Britain by over 1600 per cent in the last four hundred years. Put crudely, this means that British people today are more than 16 times better off than their ancestors living in Shakespeare's day. In the United States, the purchasing power of the average income increased between 1800 and 1990 by a factor of 30.

What makes these achievements all the more staggering is the fact that population size has multiplied at the same time as average living standards have risen. Not only is each of us much better off than we would have been two centuries ago, but there are also so many more of us sharing in this prosperity. The population of England and Wales in 1801 was 8.9 million. This number all but doubled in the next 50 years, to 17.9 million, and doubled again by 1911 to 36 million. In the twentieth century, the rate of population increase in Britain and other advanced capitalist countries has levelled off, and current low rates of fertility indicate that the total population in many countries in western Europe may even begin to fall in the twenty-first century. But as western populations stabilize, those elsewhere in the world have been spiralling upwards, for as capitalism has spread to the rest of the world, so it has sparked an even greater population boom there.

Before the advent of capitalism, the world's population was growing at an annual rate of just 0.56 per thousand. At this rate it took 1200 years for the total population of the world to double. In the two hundred years after 1750, however, the rate of increase averaged 5.7 per thousand – a rate at which total population doubled every 120 years. Since 1950, the rate of increase has averaged 17.1 per thousand, or a doubling every 40 years.[17] Among all the other things that capitalism produces, it produces the extended possibility of human life, and as with everything else that it influences, it does so at an ever-increasing rate.

The explanation for this lies in the expanded productive capacity which capitalism brings about. Increased output – including dramatic improvements in food production technologies – enables many more people to be kept alive, and improvements in sanitation, housing, medicine and other services financed out of the wealth that capitalism has generated have meant that those who are born now stand a much better chance of surviving into adulthood and of living longer than ever before. In England, the infant mortality rate (i.e. the number of babies under one year old dying per thousand live births) increased slightly in the early years of the industrial revolution and peaked in 1846–7 at 164. It then fell to 95 by 1912, to 30 by 1951, and to 12 by 1980. Coupled with this, average life expectancy rose from just 33 years in 1721 to 41 years in 1871 and to around 70 years today. The annual death rate in Britain in 1721 was 31.4 per thousand population. In 1871 it was 21.9. Today it is just 12.[18]

The myth of immiseration

Given the evidence on rising output, rising real wages, improved living standards and enhanced life expectancy, it is difficult to understand why so much of the history that is written about the development of capitalism suggests that it was an unmitigated disaster for most ordinary people. This belief seems to have originated in two sources. One is Marx's writings, and in particular his belief that as capitalism develops, the conditions of the working class become worse (the so-called 'immiseration thesis'). The other is the strong tradition of rural romanticism in English literature and drama which has often contrasted the urban squalor of the industrial proletariat and the ruthless exploitation practised by the industrial bourgeoisie with an Arcadian vision of a precapitalist 'Golden Age' in which simple peasant families lived poor but happy lives in harmony with nature, closely integrated within a small and compassionate human community. From Marx we get the idea that capitalism grinds the working population into dire poverty, and from rural romanticism we get the idea that it was all so much better in the ordered and genteel rural society of the past.

Neither of these beliefs holds up against the evidence. The early years of industrial capitalism obviously did bring enormous hardship and disruption to many people's lives as workers were forced off the land by poverty and by rural enclosures and were crowded into cramped and insanitary conditions in the rapidly expanding cities. But the conditions that they left behind were often little better than those to which they went.[19] In seventeenth-century England, the labouring population of the countryside lived in rudimentary cottages and scratched a living by cultivating a tiny plot of land, grazing a pig or cow on the common land, working for daily wages on a local estate and perhaps spinning wool for a local merchant. Their livelihoods depended crucially on the availability of seasonal work and on every member of the family toiling long hours every day. The birth of children often brought dire poverty to the family as the wife's labour was lost at the same time as another mouth required feeding, and it is estimated that at this time half of the population of England lived in intermittent, life-threatening poverty. By the age of ten, children would leave home to go into service where they would remain until they, too, married and moved into a cottage where the cycle would repeat itself. As Peter Laslett suggests, economic oppression and exploitation was a characteristic feature of rural life long before the period of industrial capitalism.

It is possible that the industrial revolution made matters even worse for a time, but from the 1820s onwards there is no doubt that the material well-being of the working population in England was slowly but irreversibly improving.[20] For all our images of the squalor of the industrial revolution, it is interesting that even Marx's collaborator, Frederick Engels, found in his review of working-class poverty in England in 1848 that the worst conditions of all were those in the countryside.[21] The loss of a rural Arcadia is a myth.

As for Marx's immiseration thesis, it is true that capitalism does create and perpetuate considerable economic inequalities between the social classes, but it also raises the living standards of rich and poor alike. For all the academic criticisms of 'trickle-down' theories of economic growth, it is clear that the enhanced wealth created by capitalism has benefited all social classes and that the luxuries enjoyed by the few in one generation rapidly became the norm for the majority in the next. Whether it be occupancy of centrally heated houses, ownership of cars and consumer durables, enjoyment of foreign holidays, access to education or provision of health care, the pattern is always the same, for capitalism thrives on mass markets and cannot survive on demand from the rich alone. Friedrich von Hayek has captured the essence of this process in the metaphor of capitalism as a column of people marching in line past a succession of fixed points.[22] Those at the front reach any given point before those at the rear, but the whole column keeps moving forward, and in a relatively short time, those at the back reach any one point which those at the front passed earlier.

Capitalism not only has raised living standards for the poor as well as the rich, but also has changed our very conception of what poverty looks like. At the turn of the century, Seebohm Rowntree conducted a famous study in the English city of York in which he drew a poverty line at the point below which families could not afford to buy the basic items of food, clothing and fuel necessary to ensure health. By 1979, Peter Townsend published a survey of poverty in Britain[23] in which he drew the poverty line at the point below which families could not afford to participate fully in a style of life which included holidays away from home, hosting of dinner parties, ownership of a refrigerator and sole use of facilities such as an indoor toilet and a bath or shower. It is indicative of the impact which capitalism has had on living standards throughout society that what we call 'poverty' today would have represented 'affluence' just a few generations earlier. Indeed, it has been estimated that people on the official poverty line in the United States today enjoy a level of purchasing power twice that enjoyed by people on average incomes at the turn of the century.[24]

A further feature of the growth of capitalism is that it has increased the opportunities available to individuals to improve their situation. Because capitalist enterprises are orientated principally to the pursuit of profit, rational employers seek to recruit and promote the most able people in the population rather than those born into particular social strata. Capitalism is by inclination meritocratic, and, as we shall see in Chapter 4, what sociologists call 'social mobility' is much more common now than in the past. Capitalism has brought with it social fluidity. The seventeenth-century rural cottagers had no realistic chance of escaping their lowly position, nor of seeing their children make any better life for themselves. This was a relatively closed social order in which half the population counted for nothing. Capitalism values individual talents and recognizes individual identities in a way that the pre-capitalist order never did.

The immiseration of the masses is one of the myths about the history of capitalism, and the destruction of a 'Golden Age' of rural Arcadia is another. Capitalism may be criticized on a variety of other grounds, but it strains credulity to accuse it of worsening the lot of the ordinary people.

The preconditions of capitalist development

In his *General Economic History*,[25] Max Weber considers and dismisses a number of factors which have been identified by historians to explain why capitalism developed in western Europe at the time that it did. Increased population in the centuries following the Black Death probably helped by creating a market for goods as well as a pool of labour; however, the population in China expanded at the same rate as in the West between 1700 and 1900 yet capitalism there 'went backwards'. Nor was the influx of precious metals from South America an adequate cause, for although these triggered an inflation in Europe in the sixteenth century which helped stimulate economic activity, they went initially to Spain and Portugal where they were squandered on military adventures and ostentatious lifestyles rather than being used for investment. Capitalism in Europe developed first not in the Iberian peninsula but in England, the Low Countries and the Italian city-states. Weber concedes that accidents of geography may have played a contributory role, for the Mediterranean Sea and a network of inland rivers made trade and communication in Europe much easier than in places like India and China, but he points out that this cannot explain early capitalist development in cities like Florence. He concludes:

> In the last resort the factor which produced capitalism is the rational permanent enterprise, rational accounting, rational technology and rational law, but again not these alone. Necessary complementary factors were the rational spirit, the rationalization of the conduct of life in general, and a rationalistic economic ethic.[26]

Weber's analysis of the origins of this 'rational economic ethic' in the Puritan religions is well known.[27] Briefly, he believed that religions such as Hinduism, Buddhism and (within Christianity) Roman Catholicism perpetuated tradition rather than challenging it, for devotees of such faiths were encouraged to look for their salvation in the next world rather than in this, and to accept their lot with good grace rather than seeking to change their condition.

Puritanism, and in particular Calvinism, was in comparison revolutionary for three reasons. First, it transformed the Catholic ethic of a contemplative vocation within a monastery by emphasizing the idea of a practical vocation in the world. It therefore created the active obligation among its followers to work to transform nature in order to glorify God, and it brought the monastic self-discipline of labour into the everyday life of ordinary people. Second, its asceticism ruled out profligacy, so that personal wealth created through devotion to labour could not be squandered on luxurious and ostentatious living but had instead to be reinvested in a further cycle of production. And third, the doctrine of predestination precluded what Calvin saw as the impertinent and blasphemous possibility of knowing and influencing God's plans for one's own salvation (e.g. through the mediation of the confessional) and therefore generated an *Angst* of uncertainty regarding this most crucial of all questions. According to Weber, this uncertainty led the Puritans to search for outward signs of their own election, and the clearest sign that they could find was worldly prosperity.

Taken together, these three factors produced an ethical culture with a close affinity to the formally rational spirit on which modern capitalist enterprise depends. As we saw earlier, production in a capitalist system is not an end in itself, but is merely a means to an end – accumulation of profit in an ever repeating cycle. For many people in the pre-capitalist world, such a system would have seemed self-evidently absurd. Why continue to work once you have created sufficient resources for your own subsistence? Puritanism made such activity meaningful.

Today, these religious underpinnings of economic activity have fallen away. Like our ancestors before Calvin's time, many of us in the established capitalist countries today may be struck by what Weber terms the 'substantive irrationality' of accumulation for its own sake. What is the point in developing a business if all you do with the proceeds is continue to expand it? Where is the sense in dedicating yourself to a career if you spend your entire life working harder and harder simply in order to achieve greater and greater advancement? If you have made your money from a business, or you have succeeded in establishing a career, why bother getting out of bed in the morning to make even more money or to drive yourself to a coronary by seeking even further advancement?

For the early Puritans, such activity had profound meaning and significance. Their religious ethic propelled them into a lifestyle of labour, accumulation and self-improvement which was precisely what was required for capitalism to flourish. Today, this religious motivation has all but vanished and we have inherited the behavioural husk having lost the spiritual kernel. We therefore continue to work methodically each day in pursuit of the next dollar, even though we may be hard-pressed to provide an adequate explanation for why we do so (see Chapter 5). This for Weber is the poignant tragedy of the modern age, that we are locked into a system which has lost its substantive meaning for us.

Weber's analysis of the role of Puritan ethics in generating the modern capitalist spirit has been exhaustively debated by historians and sociologists.[28] Some have argued that the link between Puritanism and capitalism is the reverse of that posited by Weber; that rather than Calvinism producing capitalist entrepreneurship, capitalist entrepreneurs seized on Calvinism as a self-serving justification for what they were already doing. Others have disputed the strength of the association by producing evidence that many early capitalists were not Puritans or that the working population had little commitment to these ideas even if their employers did. Fascinating as they are, however, these debates have tended to eclipse consideration of the other factors which Weber identified as necessary conditions for capitalism to develop.

Consistent with his broader sociological methodology, Weber never suggested that any one factor alone could have generated the historic changes which he devoted so much of his life to analysing and understanding. For him, history is a matter of infinite causation. In his view, it was certainly necessary for traditional culture to be radically challenged if capitalism was to take root, and given the all-pervading significance of religion in human affairs at that time, it seemed plausible to locate the sources of such a challenge in changes of religious doctrine and practice. But he also recognized that such a change could not provide a sufficient condition for capitalism to emerge. What was also necessary was a change in the social context within which economic activity was embedded.

He identified six key factors which had to coalesce before capitalism could develop and take root. It was necessary, first, that ownership of means of production came to be vested in private individuals; second, that individuals were free to trade in a market in the absence of 'irrational' constraints on their behaviour; third, that technology developed along rational lines through the mechanization of production processes; fourth, that there developed a system of formal law underpinning a predictable and rule-governed system of public administration and adjudication of disputes; fifth, that individuals were legally free and economically compelled to sell their labour without undue restrictions; and sixth, that economic life became commercialized with the recognition of rights to revenue accruing to those who provided credit or advanced share capital. These six preconditions came together uniquely in western Europe, particularly in England.

The development of capitalism in England

Some elements of modern capitalism developed earlier elsewhere, notably in the Netherlands but also in parts of Germany and in some of the Italian city-states such as Florence, Venice and Genoa, but it was in England that all the factors identified by Weber gradually came together to generate a system of production based upon capitalism.

There is no single event in English history which can be identified as decisive in this development. At one time, Marxist historians used to argue that all capitalist societies emerged out of bourgeois revolutions and that in England this turning point came in the Civil War when a rising bourgeois class based in the towns overthrew the old feudal class based in the countryside. Today, however, most historians recognize that the English Civil War was not a 'bourgeois revolution' and that Britain never witnessed a dramatic turning point equivalent to the upheavals in France in 1789.

By 1640, when the Civil War began, the rural gentry and aristocracy was already coexisting with capitalism, and there was no clear line of class demarcation between them and the wealthier urban merchants and manufacturers. They sat together in Parliament, their children intermarried, and rural landowners often invested directly in trade.[29] Nor was capitalism limited to the towns, for a capitalist system of agriculture, in which landowners rented land to capitalist farmers who in turn employed wage labour to produce food for sale in local markets, was well established by 1640. In the Tudor period, between half and two-thirds of all households in England were receiving at least part of their income from wages.[30]

The fine divisions of status which distinguished the aristocrats, the gentry and the wealthy merchants were, then, largely insignificant as compared with the bonds which united them. This made Britain unique in Europe at that time, and it rules out any simplistic analysis of the Civil War as a class struggle. The bloody battles of 1640–42 were fought between different factions of the same class who were divided by religious doctrine and political allegiance rather than by economic interest. Unlike most of Europe, the English bourgeoisie evolved in a gentrified form and the aristocracy became simultaneously bourgeois. From the mid-sixteenth century, if not earlier, there was a unified dominant class in England which was capitalistic in its orientation even if aristocratic in its lifestyle.

Rather than locating the origins of English capitalism in a clash between urban-based and rural-based property, it seems that it was precisely the unique blurring of this distinction which enabled capitalist forms of organization to evolve over time. England never developed autonomous city-states such as those in Italy, nor even major provincial towns as in France. In the seventeenth century, London was the biggest city in Europe and it contained 10 per cent of England's population, but outside of the capital there were only seven towns with a population of 10,000 or more in 1700 and they accounted for less than 2 per cent of the population.[31] England before the eighteenth century was a predominantly rural country governed from a single metropolis.

At a time when much of Europe was fragmented into princely fiefdoms and city-states struggling between themselves for autonomy and power, England was a single nation-state under the sovereign power of the Crown. There were no fortified cities and no autonomous princedoms confronting the central power, but rather several thousand tiny parishes and some 800 small market towns scattered across the country.[32] The gentry and burghers who ran these local areas relied ultimately upon the Crown for their authority.[33] Equally, royal power was never absolute, for from the time of Magna Carta, monarchic rule was mediated through this network of local ruling elites. Parliament existed to represent local ruling elites at the centre and to enable the mobilization of a consensus among them. The monarch in London could only rule the country through these local elites gathered together in Parliament, and they in turn relied for their authority upon the monarch. England never witnessed the rise of the kind of absolutist power which emerged in many other parts of Europe, for state power was always fragmented and dispersed.

If we now consider the preconditions of the rise of capitalism which Weber identified, it is apparent that England uniquely fulfilled several of them as a result of its peculiar combination of centralized order and local autonomy.

For example, Weber insists that the emergence of capitalism required 'law which can be counted upon, like a machine'.[34] The early emergence of a unified state in England provided precisely this order and predictability in law and administration. The early emergence of a rational system of law and administration dates from Magna Carta. Signed in 1215, the 'great charter' established the right of individuals to be treated according to written rules proscribing arbitrary use of arrest, imprisonment, dispossession and so on (what today would be called 'the rule of law'). This was supplemented from the thirteenth century onwards by the evolution of a system of common law involving regular assizes (in which circuit judges travelled the country trying cases in the king's name) and quarter sessions (presided over by local justices drawn from the ranks of local elites). By the time of the Glorious Revolution in the late seventeenth century, England enjoyed a system of law which safeguarded a range of individual freedoms unparalleled in the rest of Europe other than the Netherlands.[35] This system was often harsh and repressive, and it took a long time before it recognized the legal equality of all individuals irrespective of their social rank, but its essential feature was that it was relatively uniform across the country and was predictable in its application.

However, while the central power was strong enough to establish internal order and governance, it was not so strong that it could regulate local conditions of life. Within this national system of law, the jealous preservation of local autonomy opened up the possibility for trade and innovation. Two more of Weber's preconditions of capitalist development – freedom to trade and commercialization of everyday life – were thus unintentionally met as a result of the inability of the centre tightly to control and regulate local areas in England.

Trade in Europe was being opened up from the twelfth century onwards as a result of a common adherence to Christianity following the Crusades against Islam. This created the trust which was vital if merchants were to trade over long distances and to develop means of exchange (including credit) other than barter.[36] Initially, the centres for this trade were outside England in places such as Florence and the Low Countries, but as markets expanded, first within Europe and later through trade with the Americas and the East, English merchants found themselves peculiarly advantaged to exploit this expansion of commerce.

In part, this advantage stemmed from supportive action by a strong and unified state. From the Elizabethan period onwards, both Crown and Parliament equated the national interest with the defence and extension of trade. National commercial interests were safeguarded through the system of mercantilism and were extended into overseas markets by prosecuting wars and seizing colonies. All of this gave English merchants access to ever greater markets. That they were able to expand production at home to take advantage of these markets reflected the autonomy enjoyed by the localities in the countryside.

In the towns in England, as in much of Europe, day-to-day governance was vested in the guilds and corporations. The guilds established local monopolies in the right to practise certain crafts, carefully regulating entry, controlling apprenticeships and stipulating the prices and quality of raw materials and finished products. This represented an effective system of closure virtually guaranteed to choke off new developments and to stifle enterprise and initiative at birth. Throughout Europe, regulation by guilds represented a major barrier to change and an irksome restriction on the activities of merchants looking to expand production to take advantage of expanding markets.

What was different about England, however, was that the urban guilds were relatively autonomous of powerful landed interests. English landowners did try to exercise some control over neighbouring towns – e.g. by obliging bakers to use their mills, or by levying tithes and feudal dues – but the subordination of urban craftsmen to traditional rural elites was relatively weak as compared with the situation in places such as Italy where powerful noble families often controlled the towns within their areas.[37] Merchants were therefore free to build up their power in the towns by increasing their hold over local craft shops and eventually taking control of the guilds themselves. As early as the thirteenth century, merchants in England began to subordinate independent craft producers by monopolizing the supply of their materials and the marketing of their output, and by the second half of the sixteenth century, basic trades such as textiles, leather and metal goods were in most towns under the effective control of merchant guilds.[38]

It was in the rural areas, however, that the most important innovations took place. In England, the rural parishes and counties were to varying degrees under the control of local gentry and aristocrats. In the 'closed' parishes, one or two large local land-owners could regulate entry and exit and could control all activity within their estates much as the guilds were able to do in the towns. But there were also 'open' parishes in which land was dispersed over the open countryside and farmed by cottagers, squatters and small family farmers. Here there was sometimes little sign of concen-trated power. Indeed, it is estimated that around one-fifth of all parishes had no local gentry at all, and in these cases local people had effectively run their own affairs for centuries.[39]

It was to these open parishes that the merchants turned to expand their supply of manufactured goods. Rural cottagers who owned their own looms or forges were hired by merchants to produce goods which were then traded in England and overseas. By 1500, half the wool cloth produced in England came from cottage weavers based in the countryside. This 'putting-out' system was a crucial step in the development of industrial capitalism and it became widespread in England two centuries before it became established in France or Germany.[40] Only in England could merchants find in the open parishes little islands of relative autonomy from feudal rule in which they could establish new economic arrangements.

The problem with the putting-out system was, however, that it was inefficient. It entailed high costs of transportation and allowed for little direct control or coordination of the labour process. Cottage weavers could not be depended upon to continue working once they had secured an income they deemed sufficient for their needs, nor could they always be trusted not to sell some of the produce themselves. The eventual solution to this problem of labour discipline was found in the development of the factory system in which workers came to the machines and materials rather than the materials coming to the workers and their machines. The development of the modern factory system had, however, to await two more of Weber's preconditions, for it depended both on the development of rational technology and on the existence of a pool of free labour compelled by economic necessity to seek work.

The rationalization of technology dates back to before the Norman invasion. By AD 1000 four crucial technological developments had become widespread in English agriculture – the water mill for grinding corn ('Domesday Book' records 6000 mills in England in 1086), the heavy plough, the three-field system and the use of horseshoes and of new methods for harnessing animals.[41] These developments had two important features in common. First, they operated on a small scale and therefore underpinned the local economic autonomy of the village or the manor which was to become so significant later on. Second, they linked animal husbandry to arable farming and therefore favoured those parts of Europe – notably Flanders and south-east England – which offered good pasture and good arable land. The result was that productivity in these areas rose faster than elsewhere in Europe or beyond.

Technological development nevertheless proceeded slowly, and for many centuries production of both food and handicrafts was limited by the reliance upon human skill, animal power, the water mill and the use of organic material for fuel. Iron, for example, was for centuries smelted using charcoal, but the supply of charcoal depended on timber, and much of England was deforested during the Middle Ages as a result of the rising demand for fuel. This eventually sent the iron industry into decline until 1735 when a method for coking coal was discovered, and from 1740 onwards coke began to replace charcoal as a fuel in blast furnaces.[42]

The expansion of trade in manufactured goods depended upon technological innovation and before the eighteenth century it was hindered by the limited technological capacity for expanding production, and was mostly limited to supplying the military (which purchased woollen goods for uniforms and iron for cannon and firearms) and the luxury market (mainly the European royal courts and wealthy families). Industries employing heavy plant were exceptional before the eighteenth century, and most industrial production was concentrated in the craft workshops in the towns and in the cottages of rural labourers in the countryside where it was accomplished by means of rudimentary machinery such as the hand loom.

The major breakthrough came with the invention of the steam engine and its application to the manufacture of cotton goods using the Cartwright power loom of 1785. The power loom finally freed producers from the limits of a technology based on human labour power and rapidly reduced the price of cotton clothing, thereby for the first time opening up a mass market for manufactured goods both at home and abroad. In 1785 Britain imported raw cotton weighing a total of just 11 million pounds, from which it produced 40 million yards of cloth. By 1850, the country was importing 588 million pounds and was producing over 2000 million yards of cloth, over half of which was exported. Cotton alone accounted for nearly half of the total value of all British exports between 1816 and 1848.[43]

It was the invention of the steam engine which finally led to the widespread adoption of the factory system, first in cotton, then in wool, linen and silk as machines for spinning cotton were adapted for other textiles, and from thereon to other industries. Steam power was rapidly adopted for deep-seam mining (where steam engines were used to pump water from pits), in the manufacture of machine-tools (where it enabled precision engineering), and in transport (where the railways and the steam ships dramatically cut the cost of transporting bulk manufactured goods). All these developments reinforced each other. Steam pumps in the mines helped provide more coal for machines in other industries; precision engineering made it possible to manufacture railway lines on a large scale; the railways opened up markets for new manufactured goods; and so on.

World trade virtually doubled between 1800 and 1840, and English manufacturers enjoyed the lion's share of it. England exported not only manufactured goods but also the machinery which enabled other countries such as Germany and the United States rapidly to industrialize. British exports of machinery rose from under 5000 tons in 1845–9 to 44,000 tons 25 years later. As modern industrial technology spread between 1850 and 1870, so world output of coal more than doubled and that of iron quadrupled. World trade increased by 260 per cent during these 20 years.[44]

The factory system required more than just a new technology, however. It also needed a pool of free labour, people who were not bound to any rural estate or urban guild and who lacked the means to provide for their own subsistence. As we have seen, feudal ties on labour withered early in England and the wage system was widespread even in the sixteenth century. However, we have also seen how this wage system coexisted with a subsistence agrarian economy. Small farmers, cottagers and squatters supplemented wages earned from seasonal agricultural work or from the putting-out system by growing vegetables in cottage gardens, by farming strips of land laid out in open fields, or by keeping animals such as sheep, poultry, hogs or cows which they ran on common land. This system of agricultural subsistence sustained an independent peasant class which had no need to uproot itself to find work in the new industrial towns. The rural population was free to move, for feudal obligations had long since been broken, but it had no reason to move. Between 1760 and 1830, this situation changed, largely as a result of the enclosures.

The enclosure of common land had been proceeding piecemeal for several centuries, and sale and purchase of land had also resulted in some engrossing of farms through the amalgamation of smaller strips. Nevertheless, in the early eighteenth century many villages still contained large open fields and common areas of wasteland to which rich and poor alike could claim access. The open fields were divided into strips for arable cultivation, and the lord of the manor would own some of the strips which would be farmed alongside those owned by other smaller farmers and owners of cottages. The wasteland was owned by the lord of the manor, but there was a provision in the law dating back to feudal times that some of this should be made available for the use of his tenants, and cottagers also enjoyed traditional rights to graze their animals upon it, as well as to cut turf and collect fuel. Squatters who had made their homes on common wasteland away from the village also enjoyed traditional rights to cultivate and to graze their animals upon their encroachments, although they had no strips on the open fields to farm. While not every male resident enjoyed land rights under this system – farm servants, the younger sons of cottagers and recent immigrants all depended entirely upon wage labour for their subsistence – the eighteenth-century open village did contain a high proportion of inhabitants who could grow some crops and keep some animals on common land.[45]

The enclosures broke this system apart. Motivated partly by the desire for higher rents but also by a commitment to introducing more progressive farming methods, large farmers and landowners began in increasing numbers to petition Parliament for Acts of Enclosure. Between 1700 and 1760 there were fewer than 250 such Acts covering about 300,000 acres of common fields and waste, but in the next 80 years there were around 4000 Acts which enclosed over 5 million acres of common land, mainly in the Midlands. These enclosures affected approximately one-sixth of the total land area of England and Wales and changed the lives of between one-fifth and one-quarter of the rural population.

Once an Act had been passed, commissioners would visit a village to parcel out the land between all those who could demonstrate a legitimate claim. Squatters of long standing and those who owned cottages were generally given small parcels of land, but they lost their traditional rights to common pasture, and those who only rented their cottages received nothing. Individuals whose claims were recognized had to pay a share of the total legal costs of the enclosure as well as being obliged to fence their allotment, and these expenses often imposed a heavy financial burden. More significantly, the size of the plot allotted to them was generally insufficient for them to continue to keep animals, since they no longer had access to common pasture. Some of those who received small plots were able to survive, and even to expand their holdings over time. Others, however, simply sold up, recognizing that they could no longer sustain an independent subsistence.

Enclosure of common land thus helped to destroy the English peasantry and create in its place a landless proletariat. Some of those who were displaced emigrated to America. Some stayed in the villages and worked on the big farms as day labourers, relying on poor relief when no work was available. And some left the villages to seek employment in the factories which were springing up in the new industrial cities. In 1773, Manchester, with no cotton mills, had a population of 27,000. Just 30 years later, 52 mills were operating and the population had grown to 95,000. Within another 50 years, the population exceeded 300,000.[46] The steam engine provided the technology for this expansion; the assault on the English peasantry provided the labour.

The enclosures not only dispelled labour from the land, but also raised the level of agricultural productivity, for they enabled the remaining farmers to bring wasteland into production and to exploit new knowledge about fertilizers, crops and methods of husbandry which had developed from the sixteenth century onwards. English agriculture in the early eighteenth century had been extremely inefficient, for the open field system of strip cultivation effectively prevented the adoption of new techniques which needed to be applied over a whole field. Without enclosures, the rapidly growing urban population created by the industrial revolution could never have been fed. Between 1750 and 1830, however, the population of Britain more than doubled and improvements following enclosure enabled domestic farming to supply 98 per cent of the grain which these people consumed.[47]

There were, then, many unique factors which coalesced to produce industrial capitalism in England. The early unification of the nation provided a uniform and predictable system of law, and the tradition of local autonomy enabled the commercialization of economic life through the putting-out system. The existence of plentiful raw materials (especially coal) meant that the conditions were present in which new technologies such as steam power could be fully exploited. The fusion of the rural landowning and urban mercantile classes meant that the early emergence of capitalism encountered less resistance (and won more support) than elsewhere in Europe, and the breaking of the independent peasantry through enclosures provided the new industrial cities with cheap labour and cheap food. Add to all this the bonus of an overseas empire which could provide food and raw materials as well as protected markets in which to sell industrial goods, and we can begin to understand why England was so uniquely placed to become the vanguard of the new capitalist era.

Clearly the conditions under which England forged its capitalist revolution were unique. They could never be reproduced elsewhere if only because later developments in other countries have occurred in the shadow of an already existing capitalism. Germany and the United States in the second half of the nineteenth century, just like Japan and the 'little dragons' of east Asia in the second half of the twentieth century, have had to compete within (but have also been able to benefit from) a world in which capitalist enterprise has already developed. Like the first child to make footsteps in the snow, the English path to modern capitalism could never be repeated and it cannot therefore provide us with a template to which the history of other countries can be fitted, still less with a model for today's developing countries to copy. The real question for the poor countries today is whether the existence of a strong capitalist bloc of nations is more a help or a hindrance in their own attempts to find a path to capitalist prosperity, and this is the issue we consider next.

Capitalism and the Poor Countries

The poorest country in the world is probably Zaïre. The average income in Zaïre is estimated to be one-eightieth of that in the United States.[1] Zaïre is, however, only one of many countries in sub-Saharan Africa, Asia and Latin America which have hitherto failed to develop the sort of prosperity associated with capitalism in Europe, North America and Japan. Nearly 800 million people live in the mature, developed capitalist countries of western Europe, North America, Japan and Australasia. In 1990 they enjoyed an average annual per capita income of $19,900. But there are over 4000 million other people in the world who live in countries which are on average much poorer. In the Indian sub-continent alone there are 850 million people whose average per capita income in 1990 amounted to just $360.[2]

Poverty in the less developed countries

The World Bank defines poverty as 'the inability to attain a minimal standard of living'.[3] The Bank identifies two per capita income levels below which countries may be classified as 'poor'. The first and more generous poverty line is drawn at an average national income of $370 per person per year at 1985 prices. On this definition, 1115 million people – over one-fifth of the total population of the world – are living in poverty. The second line is drawn more tightly at an average income of just $275 per person per year. On this definition, 630 million people are poor. At this second level of income, poverty can be life-threatening. It is estimated, for example, that in 1980, 340 million people consumed insufficient calories to guard against stunted growth and serious risks to health.

Of course, not everybody living in poor countries is poor (just as not everybody living in the developed countries is prosperous). As in the 'developed world', so too in the 'less developed countries' (LDCs) income and wealth are unequally distributed. Approximately one-third of those living in the LDCs themselves have an income below $370, and around 18 per cent of them subsist on an income below $275 per year. The contrast between rich and poor people in poor countries can be every bit as great as the contrast between the average incomes of people living in developed and less developed countries. Nevertheless, the gap in average living standards between rich and poor countries is huge.

This gap is reflected in striking differences in life chances. The infant mortality rate in the developed capitalist countries, for example, averages 11 per thousand live births. In Latin America and the Caribbean it is 60 per thousand. In India it is 127 per thousand. In sub-Saharan Africa it is 175 per thousand. Similarly, average life expectancy in the developed capitalist countries is 76 years. In India it is 58 years. In sub-Saharan Africa it is 52 years.[4]

Contrasts of this kind lead many people to believe that the prosperity of the developed capitalist countries is in some way linked to the misery of the poor countries. How could western capitalist nations have become so rich if not at the expense of those countries in Africa, Asia and Latin America which have remained so poor? Has not the wealth of the prosperous been built upon the exploitation of the poor?

This way of thinking represents a modern version of Marx's immiseration thesis transferred to a global scale. The capitalist countries are thought to grow richer by making the poor countries poorer, and the wealthier the West becomes, the more the rest of the world is said to suffer as a result.

One way in which the rich nations are thought to prosper at the expense of the rest of the world is through their profligate use of global resources. The western economies use 80 times as much energy per head of population as the poorest countries do.[5] The implication seems to be that the poor countries are being deprived of energy while privileged westerners burn it up in their cars and factories with reckless disregard for everybody else. Similarly, western capitalist countries consume twice as many calories per person as the poor countries do, and they use food inefficiently by feeding grain to livestock. These sorts of disparities lead critics of western capitalism to draw a connection between the emaciation of fly-blown children crouching in the Ethiopian dust and the obesity of American adults strolling the shopping malls while stuffing themselves with hamburgers.

There are three major problems with such criticisms. First, they neglect to ask how all the energy, food and technology consumed by the West has been created. They focus on how the honey in the global pot is distributed without considering how it came to be in the pot in the first place. Yet it hardly makes sense to blame the poverty of the LDCs on the greed of the advanced capitalist nations if it is the latter which have developed these resources in the first place.

Second, they tend to overlook the extent to which some LDCs have pursued policies which have set back any progress towards economic development. It clearly makes no sense, however, to lay responsibility for Third World poverty at the feet of the capitalist nations if the LDCs themselves have contributed to their own misfortunes.

Third, it can be difficult to trace clear causal connections between affluence in the capitalist countries and poverty elsewhere. Where, for example, is the link between the prosperity of the Swiss (the richest nation on earth outside the oil-producing countries) and the poverty of, say, the inhabitants of Papua New Guinea (one of the poorest)?[6] Granted that we live in an increasingly interdependent world, but it is difficult to see how the Swiss can be said to have exploited the inhabitants of Papua New Guinea, for Switzerland has never even colonized another country and surely owes its affluence largely to its own efforts.

Clearly the question of whether the capitalist countries of the West became rich at the expense of the rest of the world is one which is more complex than might at first appear. There are two ways of approaching it. One is to ask whether *historically* the capitalist nations have plundered other parts of the world which remain poor today as a result of these past injustices. The obvious factors here are the history of slavery and colonialism. The second approach is to ask whether there are features of the relations between the capitalist countries and the LDCs *today* which enrich the former and impoverish the latter. This second approach will lead us to consider the role played by transnational corporations and the inequalities which might result from patterns of world trade.

Did western colonialism make the poor countries poor?

Let us first consider the history of slavery.[7] It is widely believed that Europeans introduced the slave trade to Africa and that this retarded development by removing the most economically-active people from the local populations. This, of course, could not account for the poverty of countries such as India which were never enslaved by the West. Nor could it explain poverty in eastern and southern parts of Africa, for the slave trade was concentrated on west Africa and hardly touched the eastern, central and southern parts of the continent. An additional problem is that the slave trade in Africa pre-dates the arrival of Europeans. Trading of slaves between Arab merchants and African tribal leaders had been going on for centuries before Europeans ever set foot in Africa, and it continued long after the practice was outlawed by European governments. The west African slave trade did of course bring wealth to plantation owners in the southern United States and to cotton manufacturers in north-west England, but it is difficult to maintain that it explains the subsequent economic backwardness of so much of the African continent.

If we are looking for a causal mechanism which could link the prosperity of the capitalist countries to the misery of millions of people in the LDCs, then a more plausible candidate is the history of western colonialism and imperialism. Britain, after all, was not only the world's first successful modern capitalist economy, but also the seat of the world's greatest empire, and many other successful capitalist nations, including the Dutch, the Belgians, the Germans, the Italians, the Spanish and the Portugese also had their colonies in Africa, the East Indies and South and Central America. These possessions undoubtedly did contribute to the prosperity of many of these nations, for the colonies provided cheap labour to work on plantations, supplied cheap raw materials for industry back in the 'mother country', and offered protected markets into which manufacturers could sell their goods. Although colonies also cost money in terms of administration and policing costs, they generated significant flows of revenue.

But as in the case of slavery, so too in the case of colonialism there are problems in linking current inequalities between countries to the injustices perpetrated by past plunder and conquest. For a start, not every successful capitalist nation had colonies. Many of the most prosperous capitalist countries, such as Switzerland or Sweden, never had foreign colonies, and several of them, among them Australia, Canada and the 13 original states of the USA, were themselves once colonized. Clearly, then, capitalism can prosper without the benefit of colonialism, and former colonies can prosper despite (or even because of) their historic links with an imperial power.

Furthermore, in those capitalist countries which did annex foreign colonies, economic development was obviously a precondition rather than a consequence of their conquests. For Britain to subordinate one-quarter of the world's population to its rule required the prior capacity to build ships, make maps, manufacture munitions, raise tax revenues and develop a complex system of law and social organization. A high level of economic and social development was therefore necessary before colonies could be seized, and this suggests that, rather than the Empire creating capitalist development, it was capitalist development which created the capacity successfully to colonize.

The most significant problem encountered in linking colonization to Third World poverty is, however, that the poorest parts of the world – countries such as Nepal, Liberia and Afghanistan – turn out often to be those which were never touched by colonization. One of the poorest countries in sub-Saharan Africa is Ethiopia which is also one of the few countries in that continent to have retained its independence (with the exception of just six years under Italian rule) throughout the history of colonization. Countries which were colonized have, by contrast, generally done rather better in terms of economic development than those which were not, and some of them have flourished. It is noticeable, for example, that one of the most startling examples of successful economic development since the Second World War occurred in one of Britain's last colonial possessions – Hong Kong – and that two of the other 'little dragons' of east Asia (Taiwan and South Korea) were colonies of Japan before the Second World War.

Colonization did sometimes retard indigenous economic development in the subordinated territories. India, for example, had a cotton industry of its own before the British arrived, and this was

undermined when local producers were not allowed to compete
with British manufacturers. But it also often stimulated development, for the wealth which the European colonizers sent home from
their overseas possessions was not in most cases simply 'lying
around' waiting to be seized. Crops had to be planted, mines had to
be dug, roads had to be built. And in the process of creating this
wealth, the colonizers developed the local economy.

In many areas of conquest, economic development had hardly
begun before European settlers arrived. In Australia and much of
Africa, for example, people had never seen a wheel before Europeans appeared. Throughout the colonies, European settlers
brought new agricultural technologies to areas where nomads had
previously relied upon slash and burn methods, they introduced
new crops (such as tea plants in India and rubber plants in Malaya)
which were to become major revenue earners, they built hospitals
and schools which catered to some extent for local people as well as
for the colonists, they discovered new mineral wealth and developed modern mines and oil wells to extract it, and, perhaps most
importantly of all, they brought rational systems of law and administration which (as we saw in Chapter 1) were a crucial precondition
for economic development.

For all its harshness and unfairness, therefore, the net effects of
colonization for economic development have arguably been more
beneficial than harmful. Even some Marxists now accept this, for as
Bill Warren writes: 'Direct colonialism, far from having retarded or
distorted indigenous capitalist development that might otherwise
have occurred, acted as a powerful engine of progressive social
change'.[8] The colonization of foreign peoples may be morally
indefensible by today's standards, but the fact that we find it
distasteful should not blind us to the generally positive economic
legacy which it has bequeathed.[9]

Does capitalism keep poor countries poor?

Today the colonial era is all but gone, for most European colonies
outside of the Russian Empire achieved independence in the 20
years or so following the Second World War. If colonialism really
was the factor holding development back, then we might expect that
these countries would have exploited their new-found freedoms to

develop their economies once they achieved independent nation-hood. As things have turned out, however, many of them have failed to make much economic progress since they became independent states, and some seem to have gone backwards. Furthermore, the major problems have occurred not in the immediate aftermath of independence, but ten years or more later when these nations had had time to put in place their own development strategies.[10]

Some progress has of course been made. The World Bank notes that health levels have risen dramatically in all parts of the world and that average life expectancy has increased faster in the last 40 years than during the entire previous span of human history. Mortality rates for children under five in LDCs fell from 28 per hundred in 1950 to 10 per hundred in 1990, and average life expectancy in the LDCs rose from 40 years in 1950 to 63 in 1990.[11] Nutrition has also improved. Despite a huge increase in total population size, world per capita food production increased by 12 per cent in the 20 years from the mid-1960s, and new crop strains, together with more intensive use of fertilizers, resulted in an average 2.7 per cent growth in cereal production each year between 1950 and 1985. The average daily calorie intake of the world's population increased from 2321 in 1965 to 2653 in 1986 despite the rise in the total number of mouths to feed.

World living standards have also been rising ever since the Second World War – GDP per capita rose from $2388 in 1965 to $3616 in 1989 (figures expressed in 1987 dollar values) – and many of the poorer countries have shared to some extent in this growth. Between 1960 and 1970, the economies of the poorest countries grew at an average of 3.6 per cent per annum (exports grew at over 6 per cent per annum) while middle-income countries grew at an annual rate of 5.7 per cent (with exports increasing by 7.6 per cent each year). These rates of economic growth compare with an average of 4.7 per cent per annum recorded in the developed countries, but the faster rate of population expansion in the LDCs meant that per capita income relative to that of the West worsened in many countries during this decade.

Following the oil crisis of the early 1970s and the end of the long postwar economic boom, growth rates declined in both the developed and less developed countries. On average, the economies of the developed capitalist world grew by 2.2 per cent per year between 1975 and 1990, while LDCs increased their GDP by an average of just over 1 per cent per year during this same period. Some of the poorer countries did much better than this, however. In India, the economy grew at an annual average rate of 2.5 per cent between 1975 and 1990, in south-east Asia the growth rate was 4.6 per cent per year over this same period, and in China it reached a staggering 7.4 per cent.

But other poor countries stagnated – Latin America and the Caribbean recorded zero growth over these 15 years and the countries of sub-Saharan Africa collectively recorded 'negative growth' of 1 per cent per annum over this period.[12] The Gini coefficient, which expresses degrees of inequality between countries on a scale between zero and one, rose from 0.49 in 1960 to 0.53 in 1987, indicating that the gap in per capita incomes between the richest and poorest countries was widening over this period, and World Bank projections for the 1990s suggest that sub-Saharan Africa in particular will continue to fall behind the developed world in relative terms even if it manages to achieve positive per capita growth.

Most of these countries have been independent nations for 30 years or more. Some, like the poor nations of Latin America, have been running their own affairs since the nineteenth century. Why, then, has their record of economic growth been so poor? Why did much of Latin America stagnate during the 1970s and 1980s, and why did so many African countries go backwards? Could it be that the global system of capitalism has actually been holding these countries back?

Capitalism and the 'underdevelopment' of the Third World

Until recently, many sociologists specializing in Third World development issues argued that the fundamental cause of the continuing poverty of the LDCs lay in the relations between them and the developed capitalist countries of the West.[13] They suggested that, while capitalism produced development in the rich countries, it produced 'underdevelopment' in the poor ones. The more they tried to participate in the capitalist world system, the more the poor countries were exploited by it. The problem was twofold.

First, although they were in principle 'independent', the poor nations were in reality dependent upon the West, just as they had been during colonial times. They did not enjoy effective political or economic autonomy, nor could they hope to do so for so long as western governments and western capital used local elites to help them exploit the LDCs for their own purposes. The huge transnational corporations in particular were identified as key agents perpetuating this dependency, for they often controlled budgets greater than those of Third World governments, and their decisions, made far away in Tokyo, New York or London, had enormous implications for the poor countries yet were beyond their power to influence.

This first argument therefore suggested that the economies of countries at the periphery of the world capitalist system still depended upon those at the core. They could only hope to expand if the core countries bought their exports, and they relied on the core countries to supply the capital which they needed if they were to invest in growth. This meant in practice that while some of them were starved of capital, others became entangled in massive debts, incurring huge interest payments to western banks. Whichever way they turned, the poor countries found their destinies were in the hands of the same countries which once ruled over them as their colonial masters.

One expression of this dependency was found in the operations of transnational companies in the LDCs.[14] These corporations could, it was said, roam the world setting governments against each other as they demanded tax perks and other commercial advantages as the price of their investment. Once attracted to a poor country, these companies set up branch plants there, but their decision-making centres stayed in the West and their investment and marketing strategies were driven by considerations which took little or no account of local needs. The functional interdependence of their global operations meant that their branch plants in LDCs were totally reliant upon supply of components from outside, and could be expanded or shut down with little regard for the implications for the local economy. The result was that local people and their politicians lost control of their own affairs and became fatally dependent on decisions made elsewhere.

Not only were transnational companies said to erode the autonomy of LDCs, but also their investments were seen to be of little economic benefit to the countries concerned. The scale of their operations was such that small local enterprises which already existed in these countries could not possibly compete with them so indigenous infant industries were wiped out before they could establish themselves and local markets became swamped by western goods. The profits which these companies made through their operations in poor countries were remitted back to the West, just as the colonizers before them sent their profits home, and the level of technology they employed meant that they generated only limited employment opportunities for local people. Finally, their presence in an urban centre did nothing to foster development in the surrounding rural hinterland where peasants found themselves even further exploited to supply cheap food for the urban workforces. While these huge companies might benefit a small class of local capitalists and provide some tax revenues for corrupt political leaders to squander, they therefore contributed little or nothing to the life chances of the mass of the population.

Seen like this, huge western companies function like a Trojan horse when they are invited inside the boundaries of LDCs. But this argument failed totally to address the huge benefits which can flow from such investments. Western-based multinational firms bring new technologies, new management methods, training for local workers, and contracts for local suppliers. They boost foreign earnings by increasing exports, they open up new domestic markets, they create jobs and they raise local wage levels. We shall see later that those poor countries which have managed to develop prosperous economies over the last 30 years have only done so by making use of modern technology and modern working practices and by fostering the growth of export-orientated industries. In every case, this has been achieved either by opening up their economies to investment by big western companies, or by negotiating with them to manufacture their products under licence. The countries in the Third World which have stagnated have been those which have closed their doors to foreign investment. For most LDCs today, the problem with the transnational corporations is that they do not invest enough outside the West, for three-quarters of their investment still takes place in the developed capitalist world where the major markets for their products are concentrated.

The argument that western capitalism produces 'underdevelopment' in the Third World was, however, two-pronged, and the second aspect of it had to do with the 'unequal exchange' which was said to occur between rich and poor countries in the world capitalist system.

The root causes of this unequal exchange were traced back to the days of colonialism when the poor countries were developed by the imperial powers for their own economic purposes. Infrastructure such as roads, railways and ports was laid down in the colonies to service exports to the 'mother country' rather than to facilitate production for local markets. Similarly, plantations were organized and mines were dug, but the cash crops grown on the plantations were shipped for export just as the gold, copper and other minerals produced by the mines went to the developed countries to sustain their industrial growth. When these countries achieved political independence, they therefore assumed control of economies which were orientated to the needs of the developed capitalist countries.

The result, according to these development theories, was that these countries had been locked into trading relations which offered them few benefits and little chance of expansion. Demand from the richer nations can change rapidly, and the western countries may anyway be in a position to force down the prices they pay for these goods. Producers in poor countries are thus totally dependent upon unpredictable and unstable world market prices for a narrow range of goods. When western economies enter recession, their demand for primary products used in industrial production falls, and exporting countries then find themselves facing massive reductions in foreign earnings as a result. Furthermore, because the advanced capitalist countries are constantly looking for new technologies which will reduce the cost of raw materials, LDCs can find that their foreign markets collapse as new technologies replace old ones. The development of fibre optic cable in the telecommunications industry is a case in point, for this has replaced the need for copper which was previously used as a conductor in wiring systems. This has had a drastic knock-on effect on copper-exporting nations such as Zambia, for as world demand for copper plummets, so Zambian export revenues decline and the nation's ability to buy western machinery or other goods deemed necessary or desirable for economic development is reduced.

Examples like these led many dependency theorists to argue that it was trade with the rich nations which was keeping the poor nations poor. They believed that by producing cheap exports of food and raw materials for western consumers, LDCs were effectively allowing their wealth to be siphoned away into the prosperous countries at the 'core' of the world system. Producers in the Third World were not being paid a 'fair price' for their products when they sold on world markets,[15] for they had to work much harder than their counterparts in the rich countries in order to make an equivalent return.

This argument was based on the observation that modern technology is scarce in LDCs, while labour is cheap and plentiful. Wages therefore remain low. When commodities produced in LDCs are sold on world markets, they attract a price which reflects the cheapness of the human labour which created them. Poor countries find it difficult to break out of this, for even if they invest in new machinery to raise their productivity, the powerful purchasers of their products simply push their prices further down rather than allowing them to retain the surplus. It is because these countries are poor that their goods are cheap, and because their goods are cheap, these countries remain poor.

When LDCs come to purchase goods from the West, however, the reverse situation was said to apply. Because the high-technology economies of the West are relatively efficient in the use of labour, they can pay their workers the high wages to which they have become accustomed. When they trade with LDCs, western companies therefore demand high prices reflecting the high standard of living of their workers, and if they invest further to improve productivity, the benefits are retained in the form of higher wages and higher profits rather than being passed on in price reductions.

The poor countries thus have to sell cheap but buy dear, and for as long as the developed and less developed countries produce different kinds of goods, and therefore do not compete directly with each other in the same markets, the theory held that this pattern would continue. Effectively, this meant that peasants and workers in the LDCs were transferring wealth to affluent people living in the most developed capitalist countries, and the more they produced for sale on world markets, the more they were 'exploited'.

Where this theory began to unravel, however, was in the face of mounting evidence that some poor countries were able to use their competitive advantage of cheap labour to diversify into new products which could undercut western goods in their own markets. Clearly an export-led development strategy paid huge dividends for Japan and later for the other 'little dragons' of east Asia. It was this evidence, coupled with the abysmal record of countries in Africa, Latin America and elsewhere which had tried to insulate themselves from the world capitalist system, that finally undermined the argument that poor nations remained poor because they did not have their fate in their own hands, and that they would never develop unless they uncoupled from the West and struck out on their own. Today, most development sociologists have belatedly come to recognize that the continuing poverty of many Third World countries has less to do with their contacts with the capitalist world than with their disastrous attempts to follow the advice to cut themselves off from it.[16]

Resisting capitalism

Theories of underdevelopment found a willing audience among many intellectuals and political leaders in the Third World, for these ideas not only suggested that the West was at fault for the poverty of the LDCs, but also advocated a development strategy which entailed a key role for Third World leaders to play. If the LDCs could not hope to achieve sustained and balanced economic growth for as long as they remained part of the world capitalist system, then it followed that they should break their links with this system and adopt an independent, socialist development strategy. In large parts of Latin America, Africa and Asia (including China and India), this strategy was based upon encouragement of industrialization without the aid of western technology and know-how, erection of high tariff walls against imported goods from the developed capitalist countries, and exclusion of foreign financing of investment.

As things turned out, however, when poor countries attempted to develop by delinking from the world system the results were generally disastrous. The most dramatic example was in China in the 1950s when Mao Zedong responded to his political isolation from the West and the Soviet Union by deliberately cutting his country off from the rest of the world and launching his 'Great Leap Forward' into industrialization. The result was a dramatic collapse in agricultural production as peasants were taken away from the land to work in factories with extremely rudimentary machinery, and the whole ill-fated experiment culminated in a famine between 1959 and 1962 which cost between 25 and 30 million lives.[17] Nor did this even help to create a viable industrial sector, for Chinese industry continued to produce poor-quality goods at high costs which reflected its gross inefficiency as compared with the more advanced industries in the West.

Less dramatic but similarly unsuccessful was the strategy of 'import substitution' advocated by the United Nations Economic Commission for Latin America and taken up in many parts of South America from the 1950s onwards. In the mistaken belief that countries such as Chile, Argentina, Mexico and Brazil had developed most rapidly at the times when they had enjoyed least contact with developed capitalist countries (e.g. during the two world wars), and that development had then stalled when these contacts were re-established, this strategy attempted to foster indigenous industry by erecting tariff walls to keep out cheaper western goods, taxing agriculture to subsidize infant industries, and regulating prices and wages.

These policies resulted in widespread corruption and inefficiency while overall economic growth ground to a halt. Governments in Chile, Argentina and Brazil all tried to support and protect indigenous industries in the towns while failing to reform agriculture in the countryside. This strategy created a powerful political alliance between the feudal landowners, intent on resisting land reform, and the new urban middle class, concerned to protect its salaries and profits, and this alliance looked increasingly to the state to defend its interests. The protected industries became increasingly inefficient in the absence of any competition from manufacturers abroad, and government subsidies increased in response. As the urban population grew, so the government also came under pressure to expand its own payroll in order to soak up urban unemployment and to buy off popular unrest. This simply fuelled a vicious circle in which more and more resources were siphoned away from productive investment to support a 'monstrous state apparatus',[18] and when the military dictatorships eventually took over in the 1960s and 1970s, they too used the state to maintain their position rather than to promote outward-looking industrialization. It was not western capitalism, but the state formation within these countries themselves, which blocked economic development.

In many parts of Africa, it was much the same sort of story, except that many of the countries which decided to go it alone ended up doing even worse than those in Latin America.[19] Of 31 African countries reviewed by Killick, 20 had annual average growth rates of between +1.9 per cent and −1.9 per cent between 1965 and 1989 – a significantly worse performance than elsewhere in the Third World. On average, per capita GDP in sub-Saharan Africa was no higher in 1990 than it had been in 1970, and this reflects the virtual absence of industrialization in many of these countries combined with the failure to modernize a grossly inefficient agricultural sector.

Again, this dismal record seems to have had little to do with the pernicious influence of world markets, for the terms of trade became no worse for African countries than for many others in the Third World, and in some cases world prices actually became more rather than less favourable during much of this period. During the 1970s in Tanzania, for example, the 'net barter terms of trade' (i.e. the ratio of export prices to import prices) remained at or above their level in 1960, yet the country's ability to purchase imports from its export earnings slumped by about one-third due to massive falls in the volume of production of export goods such as sisal, cotton and cashew nuts. This compares with the performance of other countries such as the Ivory Coast, Kenya and Malawi which increased their exports over this same period despite detrimental shifts in the terms of trade.[20]

The reason for the difference lies almost entirely in the different domestic policies pursued by different countries.[21] During the 1970s and into the early 1980s, GDP *declined* by an average of 0.2 per cent per year in Zaïre, by 0.5 per cent per year in Ghana, by 1.5 per cent per year in Uganda, and by 2.6 per cent per year in Chad. Agricultural production during this period fell by 0.2 per cent per year in Ghana and by 1.4 per cent per year in Mozambique. Elsewhere – in Tanzania, in Ethiopia – economies stagnated. In many of these countries, governments pursued policies which undermined domestic prosperity by damaging production of goods for export. The least successful countries have generally been those which have maintained overvalued currencies (real exchange rates in Africa appreciated by an average of 38 per cent during the 1970s, making it much more difficult for exporters to sell abroad), imposed high export taxes, and paid producers far below the world market price for their goods.

In Ghana, for example, following independence, cocoa producers were obliged to sell their crops to a state marketing board

44 *Capitalism*

which then creamed off their profits and destroyed the incentive to expand. In 1966 the Ghanaian cocoa producers received from their government just 57 per cent of the world market price for their goods. This then fell to 36 per cent in 1970, to 27 per cent in 1974 and to 15 per cent in 1979. In Tanzania, export taxes absorbed as much as 44 per cent of the sales price of coffee in the mid-1970s. And in both countries, overvalued currencies made it even more difficult for exporters to sell their goods on world markets – the IMF estimates that in the late 1970s the Ghanaian currency was appreciating at an annual rate 16 per cent faster than was warranted by the country's trade balance, while in Tanzania the figure was a staggering 92 per cent. All of this contrasts with policies in more successful African countries such as the Ivory Coast where, for example, producers of cocoa saw real prices rise by 13 per cent during the 1970s and responded by increasing production and reinvesting to generate greater efficiency.

Added to the impact of economic policies which have destroyed exports is the overall political context in many of these countries. As in Latin America, political corruption is rife and debilitating in some African countries, and public administration is chaotic or grossly inefficient in many others. Governments have sought to maintain their position by granting privileges to inefficient urban-based industry and commerce and by expanding the public sector payroll, and to pay for this they have used the state marketing boards to loot the agricultural economy.

On top of all this, civil wars in various parts of Africa have torn some countries apart, military coups and counter-coups have been commonplace, and some countries, such as Uganda under Idi Amin, have systematically expelled or exterminated the very entrepreneurs and intellectuals on whom the future possibility of development depended.[22] Governments have taken economic surpluses which could have financed new investment to pay instead for hugely expensive prestige projects. They have neglected the infrastructure inherited from colonial times, have actively discouraged investment by multinationals by nationalizing those already there, and have undermined indigenous local enterprises by smothering them with petty regulations or by submerging them under grandiose bureaucratic economic plans which came to nothing. If a rational, settled and predictable context of law and administration is a crucial precondition of capitalist development, it has been conspicuously absent in many of these countries in the period since independence.

Embracing capitalism

Perhaps the major problem with the underdevelopment thesis was that it never satisfactorily explained what there was to stop Third World producers from diversifying away from their primary exports and using their cheap labour to compete directly in world markets for manufactured goods. An export-led development strategy did not have to rely on traditional exports, but could start to develop new ones. Armed with modern technology and cheap labour, producers in LDCs could soon be expected to undercut competitors in the developed countries and to make inroads into their markets, thereby accumulating revenues which could cover the cost of necessary imports of western capital goods while rapidly lifting these countries out of poverty. Rather than cutting themselves off from the world in order to conserve precious foreign exchange, why not go out into the world in an attempt to earn it?

This, of course, is precisely what the successful east Asian economies began to do from the 1960s onwards, for countries such as South Korea and Taiwan followed the earlier example of Japan by deliberately targeting export markets where they believed they could undercut existing western suppliers. In this way, countries which only a generation ago were poor and could seemingly be written off as hopelessly 'dependent' on the West[23] have now emerged as vibrant industrial trading nations whose economic strength is posing a major threat to the established capitalist countries.

It has often been argued that 'latecomers' to industrialization are disadvantaged in the world capitalist economy relative to those countries which are already established. Poor countries which attempt to industrialize are said to be hampered by their tiny domestic markets and find that they cannot penetrate the tariff barriers protecting more lucrative foreign markets. They also lack access to capital and their initial low rates of productivity mean they generate only small surpluses to reinvest while firms in established countries have huge turnovers and can plough vast sums back into production. They cannot therefore hope to compete successfully with the established centres of capitalist activity, for they face obstacles to development which are much more severe than those successfully overcome by countries such as Britain, Germany and the United States which industrialized much earlier.

What this analysis ignores is the crucial advantage that 'latecomers' enjoy by their opportunity to benefit almost immediately (assuming they choose to do so) from technologies which took many years to evolve in countries which industrialized earlier. From the time when Britain first began to industrialize at around 1780, it took nearly 60 years for output per head of population to double. In the United States, where industrialization began about 60 years later than in Britain, it took nearly 50 years for per capita output to double. In Japan, which began industrialization in 1885 or thereabouts, it took about 34 years. In Brazil it took just 18 years from 1961. In South Korea it took only 11 years from 1966. China doubled its output per head in just ten years from 1977.[24] The more technology advances, the more rapidly it can raise output and living standards once it is introduced into a backward economy.

But if diffusion of technology is the key to Third World development, this necessarily entails active participation in world trade. Those countries which since the Second World War have escaped poverty and developed modern economies with rapidly rising living standards have been those which have embraced capitalism by welcoming foreign investment and building up industries which have been able to compete successfully for export markets. Those countries which, conversely, have followed policies of import substitution and of disengagement from the world system, or which have relied upon socialist controls such as licensing of production and determination of price and wage levels, have stagnated.

The 1987 World Bank report allocated 41 LDCs to one of four categories depending upon the degree to which their policies emphasized an 'outward' or 'inward' orientation in relation to trade with the rest of the world.[25] Countries with a strong outward orientation included South Korea, Singapore and Hong Kong. Brazil, Malaysia and Thailand were included in the group of countries with a 'moderate' outward orientation, while Kenya, Nicaragua and the former Yugoslavia were found to have a moderate inward orientation. Countries with a strong inward orientation (characterized by extensive use of protectionism, regulation of imports by quotas and licences, and overvaluation of exchange rates) included Argentina, Bangladesh, Tanzania and Zambia. The report found that in the period 1963–85, real annual growth of GDP averaged 8 per cent (6 per cent per capita) in the outward-orientated countries as compared with just 3 per cent (1 per cent per capita) in the inward-orientated ones.

This sort of evidence suggests that the most successful development strategies are those which open countries up to the world capitalist system. Not socialist planning but global capitalism seems to offer the key to growth and prosperity. The contrasts between South and North Korea, the postwar West and East Germanies, Taiwan and the People's Republic of China, Japan and India, all speak to the superiority of capitalist over socialist development strategies.

The clearest example of this is Hong Kong, where successful capitalist development has been based largely on the classic liberal principles of minimal government involvement.[26] This is a tiny city-state of 400 square miles which has a population density 14 times greater than that of Japan. With no natural resources, energy supplies and even water have to be imported. Despite these disadvantages, the colony has developed a thriving capitalist economy under the benign influence of a British colonial administration. In the 1970s the GNP of Hong Kong grew at an annual average rate of nearly 9 per cent. Between 1960 and 1980, as the population of the colony increased by nearly 3 per cent each year, per capita GNP nevertheless grew by 7 per cent per annum. In 20 years, the population increased by 50 per cent yet real wages doubled and there was virtually no unemployment. All of this was achieved by following a *laissez-faire* policy of no exchange controls, no import tariffs, no restrictions on imports and exports, no special incentives for investors, no regulations governing local participation in foreign companies, no minimum wage laws, no price controls, and only minimal government involvement in commerce. Industry and commerce in Hong Kong operate in the context of a genuinely free market.

Even in Hong Kong, however, the colonial administration is involved in provision of comprehensive primary education, subsidized housing accommodating around half of the population, and extensive public health services. Furthermore, the Hong Kong case is in many respects exceptional, for, as we shall see, all the other east Asian examples of successful, outward-orientated development strategies have entailed a positive role for government in the economy.

The first country in the Far East to develop rapidly was Japan, which began to industrialize in the late nineteenth century and which took off into rapid growth during the 1950s when GNP tripled under a sustained average annual rate of growth of 9 per cent. By 1970 Japan had become one of the world's major industrial producers with a standard of living at least comparable to that of the older developed capitalist nations. This was then followed by South Korea, where the economy grew at an annual rate of 10 per cent between 1963 and 1974 and GNP tripled; Taiwan, where GNP rose 11-fold between 1952 and 1980; and Singapore, where GNP rose by more than 8 per cent per year between 1955 and 1974.

Today, other countries in the region – Thailand, Malaysia and Indonesia – show similar signs of rapid development. Malaysia, for example, has recorded five successive years of annual growth in excess of 8 per cent and is now the world's leading exporter of computer chips and the third largest producer of semiconductors. Electronic goods have now replaced textiles as the country's principal export.[27] These three most recent success stories, together with Japan and the four 'little dragons', have between them re-corded an average annual rate of growth (per capita GNP) of 5.5 per cent over the period from 1965 to 1990. This growth rate is more than double that achieved by the OECD advanced capitalist nations in the same period; is three times that achieved in southern Asia and Latin America; and is more than 25 times greater than the average growth rate in sub-Saharan Africa.[28]

Elsewhere in Asia, China is emerging as a major industrial nation of the twenty-first century following the effective abandonment of central planning since 1977. The decollectivization of agriculture in 1978 doubled grain output in just five years, and during the 1980s further deregulation of industry and commerce helped increase China's GNP at an annual rate of 9.5 per cent.[29]

What do these countries have in common? To some extent, of course, they may be said to share a broadly common culture, very different from that in the West, but nevertheless valuing practicality and pragmatism, emphasizing an active orientation to life, an interest in material things and an acceptance of deferred gratifi-cation and individual self-discipline.[30] Peter Berger points out that, despite the conservatism of Confucianism and the other-wordliness of Buddhism, the east Asian cultures do seem broadly consistent with the spirit of capitalism, even though they are very different from Calvin's Protestant ethic. The major difference is that the Protestant emphasis on individualism is in these countries replaced by strong group identities and a commitment to hierarchy and communal authority. As we shall see in Chapter 5, this sort of collectivism may in fact be better suited to the conditions of modern corporate capitalism than is American-style individualism.

It is not only the culture, however, which explains the success of these countries. Their record since the 1960s also has a lot to do with the policies adopted by their governments. With the sole exception of Hong Kong, these countries have not embraced unfettered capitalism, for their governments have played a key role alongside the private sector. In all of them, government provided a stable and secure system of public administration and law and order (often, it has to be said, by means of non-democratic, authoritarian regimes). In all cases, too, measures were adopted to spread some of the benefits of growth to the poorer sections of the population (e.g. through land reforms in South Korea and Taiwan; through mass housing programmes in Singapore and Hong Kong; and through support of rice prices in order to raise rural incomes in Indonesia).[31] Most, however, have gone beyond this, for governments have also become involved in various ways in managing aspects of the economy.

We should not be surprised about this. We saw in Chapter 1 that the English take-off into industrial capitalism was achieved with the help of a supportive state which not only secured a strong basis of law at home, but also extended and defended markets overseas and pushed through 'land reform' (in the form of enclosures) which raised agricultural productivity. Germany then industrialized in the second half of the nineteenth century by erecting high tariff walls designed to protect its own 'infant industries' against competition from British manufactures while at the same time allowing imports of capital goods from Britain so that German factories could have access to the most efficient machinery. The German government under Bismarck also developed a social security system designed to provide support for the poor during the period of transition, and sponsored land reform designed to break the feudal power of the *Junker* class in Prussia. At around the same time, the Japanese similarly used the power of the state to help modernize the country following the Meiji restoration of 1868. The feudal aristocracy was stripped of its fiefdoms, new government enterprises were established which were later sold off to Japanese nationals once they had become established, people were sent to the West to learn about new methods of production, and a universal system of state education was set up as an investment in 'human capital'.

The point about these early examples of state-supported economic development is that they went with the grain of capitalism rather than against it. The same has been true of the twentieth-century 'miracles' in east Asia. As in Britain, Germany and Japan, industrialization was preceeded by land reform (in the case of Taiwan and South Korea, the power of the landowners was broken by Japanese colonization before the Second World War). All of these countries also built their industries on foreign technology (Hong Kong, Singapore, Malaysia and Indonesia all opened themselves up to direct foreign investment, while Japan, South Korea and Taiwan achieved access to foreign technology through licensing). Most of them targeted key export industries which were given automatic access to cheap credit and which were further aided by government export marketing agencies, government-funded research, government training schemes for workers, and high protective tariffs against foreign imports which threatened infant industries. But in all cases, the pattern of state intervention was guided by the logic of the market – it was 'market-friendly'.[32]

Tightly monitored performance criteria ensured that subsidies were not wasted on uncompetitive or inefficient industries, and competition in foreign markets ensured that these industries remained efficient. Strict budgetary discipline (including balanced budget laws in Indonesia and Thailand) kept a cap on the level of subsidies to prevent public spending from spiralling upwards and crowding out private investment. Taxes were kept low in order to maintain incentives, and none of these countries was seduced into developing comprehensive welfare systems on the western European model. There have been no minimum wage laws, no attempts at price regulation, no crippling levies on exporters, and no strategy to redistribute wealth away from high earners.[33] Nor have these governments generally tried to run industries themselves. Relations with private sector business are close, but these governments have generally been facilitative rather than directive, aiding fledgeling companies until they are able to establish a competitive advantage in world markets rather than pushing investment into sectors where government wanted growth to occur.[34]

This pattern of state involvement contrasts vividly with that found in poor countries which have failed to develop. The essence of the east Asian strategy has been support for export-led growth, an emphasis on participation in world markets, a willingness to accept foreign capital where it can help domestic production to expand, and a commitment to taking on and beating existing capitalist producers in their own markets. The bankrupt strategy of development through import substitution which has bedevilled so much of Latin America, Africa and southern Asia was in east Asia dropped very early on.

There are signs that some poor countries have begun to assimilate these lessons. India, which for years pursued a strategy of economic self-sufficiency involving bans on foreign investment, centrally planned industrialization and tight regulation of trade, hit an economic crisis in 1991 in which growth came to a halt, inflation spiralled and the budget deficit grew to 9 per cent of GNP. Since then, taxes have been cut, industrial licences have been pruned, foreign investment has been encouraged, and the currency has been made semi-convertible. By 1994, foreign currency reserves had grown to $13 billion, inflation was back in single figures, growth was running at 4 per cent per annum, and Coca-Cola was on sale in the streets of Delhi.[35] In Latin America, too, countries such as Brazil, Chile and Argentina have now abandoned their insular economic strategies with encouraging results, and in Africa, countries such as Zambia and Tanzania have turned away from the socialist programmes of the post-colonial era and are now privatizing some of their state-owned industries and even establishing stock exchanges.

There seems no reason why the remarkable achievements of the capitalist countries of east Asia since the 1950s could not be emulated in other countries today, although the GATT agreement of 1993 now makes it more difficult to protect infant export industries than it was in the past. The success of Japan and the four 'little dragons' demonstrates that capitalism can spark rapid and dramatic growth in the less developed parts of the world today just as it unleashed unprecedented productive forces in Europe two hundred years ago, but it can only do so if governments are willing to let it happen. The major barrier to Third World development in the post-war years has not been the nature of the world capitalist system, but the inability or unwillingness of some Third World governments to take advantage of the opportunities which this system offers.

3
Capitalism and the Environment

Capitalism, we have seen, is a growth machine. Competition between capitalist producers stimulates perpetual innovation. The result is that basic resources such as food and clothing come to be produced in ever greater quantities at ever reduced costs while new luxury items become commonplace within the space of a generation. Average living standards are thus perpetually transformed. Across the world, per capita incomes rise even as total populations expand. It is as if we have come into possession of the alchemists' secret of how to turn base metal into gold.

During the last third of the twentieth century, however, there has arisen a critique of capitalism which sees this discovery of the secret of seemingly perpetual growth as a curse rather than a benefit for humankind. Finding its clearest expression in sections of the 'deep green' movement,[1] this critique accepts that modern capitalism is indeed a growth machine, but argues that this is precisely what is wrong with it. Where, it asks, is the advantage in a system which can sustain huge rates of population growth if the planet is already dangerously overcrowded? How can it make sense for Third World countries to follow a path of capitalist industrialization when existing levels of industrial production in the developed countries are already exhausting world supplies of energy? How can capitalism be permitted to go on expanding and growing when the ecosystem on which we all depend is already near the point of collapse? How can we tolerate capitalism's perpetual search for technological innovation when new technologies have already brought us to the precipice of global annihilation?

The environmental limits to growth

Economic development has always involved transformation of the natural environment, but in the last two hundred years the pace of development has quickened, and the relationship between human beings and the natural environment has changed fundamentally as a result.

One aspect of this change is that we have extended our control over the natural environment. Two hundred years of industrial capitalism have harnessed and tamed nature. This has brought obvious benefits, for people living in the developed capitalist nations no longer inhabit a world where their existence is daily threatened by famines, plagues, floods, droughts and other contingencies of nature, while even in the Third World, mortality rates have dropped dramatically. The environment in which we live has been made more controllable than ever before.

In another sense, however, nature now seems more threatening than ever before. The more we have extended our control over nature, the more we have brought about changes in the environment whose effects may be unpredictable. We have altered nature in ways which we do not fully comprehend, and as the pace of change speeds up, so the impact of our activities becomes ever more marked, for ecosystems cannot adjust quickly enough to accommodate all the changes wrought by industrialization over the last two hundred years. In many instances we simply do not know how much damage we are causing, how serious it is, and how long it might take to reverse it. We live in an age of high rewards but high risk.

The deep green critique of capitalism holds that this gamble with the future of the world is no longer worth the risks involved and that industrial capitalism must therefore now be replaced by an entirely different economic and social system underpinned by a very different set of values:

> Our current industrial way of life is too far gone. It is not a question of nearing the abyss; we daily look down into it . . . It is not so much decapitation that we should be aiming at as the decommissioning of the entire monster.[2]

In this view, the continued pursuit of growth in the West, coupled with the desire of the LDCs to emulate western living standards, can only lead to global disaster. The 1987 report of the World Commission on Environment and Development (the Brundtland

Report) suggested that bringing LDCs up to the existing living standards in the developed countries would involve a fivefold increase in current levels of energy consumption, yet even a doubling of energy consumption would create a major crisis of global warming and acidification of rainfall.[3] The implication drawn by many greens is that the global ecosystem can only tolerate even limited Third World development if there is substantial and simultaneous deindustrialization in the West.[4]

Capitalism thus stands condemned, not for its failure to raise living standards, but for its success in so doing. The triumph of capitalism at the end of the twentieth century turns out to have been a Phyrric victory, for what capitalism does best – stimulation of rapid growth – is what the world can no longer afford. The future of our planet is apparently threatened by overpopulation, melting ice-caps, rising skin cancers, declining resources and a collapsing ecosystem, and most or all of this is the by-product of capitalism's success in generating economic growth.

Because nobody of goodwill could possibly desire such outcomes, greens tend to find a receptive audience for their ideas, particularly among the young. Green ideas, dimly understood, are nevertheless widely endorsed, for it seems only common sense to draw back from activities which threaten the destruction of the planet. The green agenda seems almost 'beyond politics', something which no sensible person could possibly oppose. Environmental education is even taught now in primary schools, and many teachers are apparently sympathetic to the green movement.[5] Yet this agenda is deeply political. Greens invite us to endorse policies which would lead to dramatic changes in our economic, social and political systems. So-called 'deep greens' in particular seek the power to control, regulate, limit, ban or even reverse the technological development which has made economic growth possible in the past. They seek to bury the Victorians' faith in progress and to foster a temerity about future development. Their enthusiasm is for turning back, not going on. The capitalist growth machine is represented by them as a monster created by Frankenstein, something powerful, out of control, destructive and seemingly uncontainable. Rather than celebrating it, as the Victorians did at the Great Exhibition, they exhort us to kill it off. For while it is true that not all greens are opposed in principle to capitalism, many aspects of the green programme represent a fundamental challenge to some of the most basic features of a modern, industrial, capitalist economy.

Is there an environmental crisis?

Green critiques of capitalism range over a variety of loosely connected issues. Among the most important are the problems of world population growth, resource depletion, pollution and the disposal of waste, and the apparent onset of global warming and destruction of the ozone layer consequent upon increasing levels of industrial activity. Some of these turn out to be genuine problems; others are not.

The estimated total *population* of the world in 1900 was 1630 million, of whom around one-third lived in the 'developed' industrial nations.[6] By 1950 the total had risen to 2516 million, and around one-third still lived in the developed countries. In the second half of the century, however, the rate of population growth in the LDCs began to outstrip that in the developed world, and by the year 2000 it is predicted that total world population will have increased to over 6000 million, 80 per cent of whom will be living in Third World countries. The Brundtland Report further predicts that, at current growth rates, the global population will reach between 8 and 14 billion by 2100, with about six out of every seven living in the poorer nations.

Concern about this escalating rate of population growth in the Third World has been at the heart of the green agenda since the movement first appeared in the 1960s. At that time, the worry was that there would soon be too many mouths to feed. As things have turned out, however, introduction of new agricultural technologies have kept increases in cereal production well ahead of increases in population, with the result that today starvation in Third World countries tends only to occur as a result of calamities such as floods and civil wars.

The fact that capitalism has proved that it can feed the world has not, however, reduced green concerns about increasing population. Rather, the argument for tighter population controls has shifted from the threat of food shortages to a broader concern about 'sustainable development'.

The concept of 'sustainable development' was introduced in the 1987 Brundtland Report as the touchstone for a world economic and environmental strategy. Essentially it is the principle that the present generation should leave to its children a legacy of natural and humanly-produced assets which is no more depleted than the one it received from its parents. According to the Brundtland Report, current rates of population growth fly in the face of this principle because they are placing too great a strain on the natural environment. Future generations will suffer as a result of our irresponsible fecundity.

The report points out that industrial production has increased by a factor of 50 in the last hundred years and that four-fifths of this increase has come since 1950. Given that Third World countries are trying to catch up with the West, we can expect industrialization to increase still further in the coming years. Even at stable population levels, this implies a huge rise in pollution and energy consumption, but with the world's population expanding as it is, the demands upon global resources will become intolerable. It follows that sustainable development cannot possibly be achieved if world population continues to escalate, and the report therefore stresses the need for 'urgent steps' to limit future population growth in the Third World where the problem is most acute.

The more radical fringes of the green movement go much further than this, however. Some 'deep greens' have likened human life to a bacillus, reproducing and taking over the world, and they have proposed draconian remedies to 'cure' it. Even in Britain, where population size is static, the Green Party proposed legislation in the 1980s to limit the right to have children, and many greens apparently believe that the country's population needs to be halved.[7] Such a dramatic reduction could, of course, only be achieved through the adoption of highly coercive measures, for even the Maoist dictatorship in China failed to reduce population levels despite imposing a quota of one child per family. Recognizing the problems, a leading figure in Friends of the Earth has proposed a Huxleyian vision of state-licensed baby production as the solution: 'Childbearing [should be] a punishable crime against society unless the parents hold a government licence . . . All potential parents [should be] required to use contraceptive chemicals, the government issuing antidotes to citizens chosen for childbearing'.[8] Extreme measures like this are defended on the grounds that the future of the planet is at stake, and dramatic steps are therefore necessary. Not for the first time in history, radicals with a vision are happy to justify their means by their ends.

This strong commitment to cutting population levels is linked to the second feature of the green agenda which involves reducing the use of *natural resources*. Back in 1972, the Club of Rome published a report which predicted that some crucial raw materials were about to be exhausted. World reserves of natural gas would be used up by 1994; the petrol pumps would run dry in 1992; copper and lead would run out by 1993; and so on. No matter how they manipulated their computer projections, industrial capitalism seemed destined to hit the buffers some time in the next century.[9]

As with the earlier worries about impending food shortages, the fears of the Club of Rome regarding resource depletion soon proved groundless. The resources which the report identified as in terminal decline are more plentiful today than they were when it was written, and this reflects the remarkable adaptability of the capitalist market system to changes in its external environment. The prospect of energy shortages, for example, raised the price of oil and gas, and this stimulated companies to explore in new areas, to develop new extractive technologies, to develop substitutes, and to improve efficiency in their use of energy. Nobody today is talking any longer about basic raw materials running out.

The green response to this has been to shift the focus of attention on to threats posed to other types of resources. One which has received particular attention is the tropical rainforest of the Amazonian basin. This and the world's other rainforests currently extend over more than 1000 million hectares of land, but about 8.5 million hectares (or around 1 per cent) are on average being cleared each year, and it is estimated that well over 400 million hectares may already have disappeared, largely as a result of enroachments by Brazilian cattle ranchers.[10]

The rainforests are thought to be crucial for global ecology for two reasons. First, they convert carbon dioxide into oxygen and therefore help counter the build-up of CO_2 in the atmosphere. Second, they are thought to be the natural habitat for millions of species of plants and animal life, as yet undiscovered and unclassified. As forests are cleared, so species are (presumably) wiped out, thereby depriving us of potential sources for new drugs and cures which we cannot today anticipate. The 1994 UN Environment Programme's report estimates that between 2 and 8 per cent of the world's species are likely to be wiped out in the next 25 years if this rate of clearance continues, and, according to Friends of the Earth, one species is becoming extinct every 30 minutes. As Robert Whelan points out, however, there is an Alice in Wonderland quality to attempts to estimate the rate of extinction of species when we do not even know whether they exist in the first place.[11]

The world's forests are not only under threat from Amazonian bulldozers, however. In parts of Europe, acid rain is thought to be responsible for killing trees in the Black Forest and in parts of Scandinavia as well as for poisoning lakes and wiping out fish stocks. The acidity of the rainfall is in turn attributed by some scientists to the build-up in the atmosphere of sulphur dioxide as the result of sulphur emissions from coal-burning power stations.[12]

This is just one example of the third area of green concern, namely, the contamination of nature by the *disposal of waste products* into the air, the sea or the ground. In capitalist societies, it is argued, the emphasis on profitability and cost efficiency leads to a disregard for problems of disposal of waste products. Private profit is put before the general good, and the prospect of immediate gain is allowed to eclipse concern about future dangers.

Oil companies, for example, seek to sell more petroleum and car makers look to sell more cars, but both fail to take into account the increase in noxious emissions from car exhausts or the loss of countryside to new motorways. In many of the world's cities – Los Angeles, Mexico City, Athens – emissions from car exhausts have created poisonous smogs resulting in increasing levels of bronchial diseases, but manufacturers keep turning out more cars.

Manufacturers compete for customers by using extravagant packagings for their products or by developing 'convenience' products (such as disposable nappies) which can be thrown away after use, but the result is a mountain of rubbish, much of which will never naturally biodegrade even after years of lying buried in landfill sites. There is today a major problem of disposing of non-degradable and non-recyclable rubbish. Yet every year, the average American generates another half a ton of garbage.

Farmers seek to raise crop yields by spraying toxic pesticides on their crops and by feeding the land with nitrates, yet these chemicals then seep into the water supply, contaminating rivers and underground aquifers. Many of the world's rivers can no longer cope with the levels of industrial effluent discharged into them, with the result that fish life has been extinguished beneath a surface froth of chemical slime, and along the North Sea and Mediterranean coasts bathing beaches have become so contaminated that swimming is regarded as hazardous to health.

In most of these cases, damage continues to be inflicted upon the environment as a result of a competitive capitalist system in which producers seek to expand their markets and reduce their costs, but do not have to take account of the pollution that they cause. By and large, pollution costs do not appear on company balance sheets, nor even in government accounts, for these are costs which are rarely itemized and rarely represented in terms of money values. The New Economics Foundation has estimated that the 'externality costs' incurred by the community at large as a result of air and water pollution in Britain could add up to more than £21,000 million each year, equivalent to 6 per cent of GDP,[13] but these costs are routinely disregarded in capitalist accounting practices.

The fourth, and currently most pressing, area of green concern has to do with two potentially catastrophic changes in the *Earth's atmosphere*. The first is the apparent rise in global temperatures which is said to have been brought about by increased emissions of so-called 'greenhouse gases' from the burning of fossil fuels. The second is the appearance of 'holes' in the ozone layer over the poles which are attributed to increased emissions of chlorofluorocarbons (CFCs) used in refrigeration, air-conditioning systems and aerosol sprays.

If true, both of these developments could be extremely serious. Greens warn that global warming threatens to melt the eastern Antarctic ice-cap and raise sea levels by as much as 6 or 7 metres, thereby flooding vast areas of low-lying land across all continents. The British environmental group, Ark, predicted in 1989 that the eastern coastal towns of Grimsby, Great Yarmouth and Hull would all be under water by the year 2050.[14] Meanwhile, destruction of the ozone layer threatens to expose us to harmful radiation from the sun and thus to precipitate a dramatic rise in skin cancers and possible damage to crops.

As with many other aspects of the green agenda, however, the evidence on which these predictions are based is bitterly contested. As regards global warming, for example, nobody denies that the amount of carbon dioxide and other 'greenhouse gases' in the atmosphere has risen by as much as 50 per cent since the beginning of the industrial revolution.[15] There is, however, widespread disagreement about whether global warming is occurring, whether the build-up of CO_2 is responsible for any rise in temperatures which may be occurring, and whether any of this really matters.

The data on global temperatures over time are notoriously unreliable, for most sampling points are based in urban areas which are warmer than the rest of the Earth's surface. A study of ocean temperatures by researchers at Massachusetts Institute of Technology found no significant rise in temperature between 1856 and 1986, and a study based solely on rural measurement stations in the USA found a *fall* in average temperatures of 0.15 degrees Celsius between 1920 and 1990. Satellite data indicate only a tiny rise (just 0.1 degrees Celsius) in average global temperatures between 1979 and 1992.[16] As far as we can tell, global temperatures seem to have fallen in the late nineteenth century, risen between 1900 and 1940, fallen again up to 1965, and to have risen sharply since then. Taking the twentieth century as a whole, it is unlikely that average temperatures have risen by more than 0.5 degrees Celsius.[17]

If some warming is occurring, it is by no means clear that it is due to increased emissions of greenhouse gases generated by human activity. In 1992, world leaders met in Rio de Janeiro and agreed to combat the threat of global warming by reducing carbon emissions to 1990 levels by the end of the decade; in 1994, a report by a UN panel investigating climate change suggested that this target was inadequate and that carbon emissions needed to be reduced by 60 per cent if the world's climate was to be stabilized.[18] Yet some scientists believe that the build-up of carbon dioxide is having little effect on the earth's climate since it is triggering feedback mechanisms which re-establish an equilibrium. Furthermore, if the build-up of CO_2 really was causing global warming, then, according to most computer models, there should already have been a much greater rise in temperatures than has in fact occurred.[19] Some scientists have begun to suspect that temperature fluctuations may have more to do with volcanic eruptions or sunspot activity than with the build-up of carbon dioxide.[20]

Even if temperatures are rising, it need not follow that this is so serious as to warrant dramatic reductions in industrial activity in order to correct it. An increase of 2 degrees Celsius would bring us back to the average temperature levels in AD 1200. This would harm some regions, such as the US grain belt, but would benefit others, including Mexico, India and Africa, where increased rainfall would help agriculture.[21] And if the Antarctic ice-cap (which at present is actually expanding) began to melt, it could take another 6000 years for sea levels to rise by the 6 or 7 metres which Ark was forecasting in the late 1980s when it warned of widespread flooding within two generations.[22] Currently, sea levels are rising at a rate of just 1.8 millimetres per annum.

Fears about global warming may, therefore, have been exaggerated. Some scientists believe that the same could be true of the problems with the ozone layer.

A 'hole' in the ozone layer over the Antarctic was first discovered in 1985, and in 1989 another 'hole' was found appearing sporadically over the Arctic. Since then, however, it has become clear that the thickness of the ozone layer fluctuates naturally between night and day and between the seasons, for the stronger the sun shines, the more ozone is produced.[23] A 'hole' in the ozone layer appears regularly for a few weeks over the Antarctic at the end of the southern winter until stronger sun produces more ozone. In some years this hole is larger than others (in 1988, for example, it was less than one-fifth the size it had been in 1987).[24] It is by no means clear that ozone thickness is depleting consistently over time.

Nor is it clear that CFCs are responsible for the ozone depletion which may be occurring. We know that chlorine does break down ozone and the theory is that CFCs in the atmosphere shed their chlorine compounds and thus destroy the ozone layer. The evidence that it is CFCs that are doing the damage is, however, shaky. World production of CFCs peaked in the 1980s at 1.1 million tonnes per annum. This compares with the 300 million tonnes of chlorine evaporating annually from the sea, the 1000 tonnes of chlorine emitted every day for the last hundred years by Mount Erebus, and the 289 billion kilograms of hydrochloric acid (570 times greater than the total annual world production of chlorine and fluorocarbon compounds) spewed into the atmosphere by the eruption of a single Alaskan volcano in 1976.[25] As with global warming, so too with the ozone layer, the impact of human activity upon the atmosphere seems tiny when compared with the effects of natural forces.

Despite these doubts, however, over 50 governments signed the Montreal Protocol in 1988 which committed the developed nations to reducing their CFC emissions by 50 per cent (later raised to 85 per cent) by 1998, with less tight limits being imposed on LDCs. Both the USA and the European Union have subsequently announced a complete ban on CFCs by the year 2000, thereby necessitating the development of more expensive and often less efficient substitutes.

The main reason for the ban is that western governments are concerned about a rise in the incidence of malignant melanoma among their (largely fair-skinned) populations. The most significant cost of phasing out CFCs falls, however, on the Third World. In the tropics, CFCs are routinely used as cheap and efficient means of refrigeration for food and medicines, and because they are simple chemicals they can easily be manufactured locally. Replacements are less efficient, are often toxic (and therefore dangerous to the health of those handling them), and can only be made under licence from large western chemical companies (which makes them more expensive). International action on the ozone layer has therefore imposed new costs on countries which can ill afford them.

The irony in all this is that there is no compelling evidence that CFCs are doing much if any damage. While it is true that the ozone layer helps protect us from ultraviolet radiation from the sun, measurements at sea level of ultraviolet B reveal a decrease in recent years of between 0.5 and 1 per cent per year, and UV intensities in American cities were lower in 1985 than in 1974.[26] It is difficult to see how data like these can be reconciled with the claim that CFC emissions are responsible for the increasing incidence of skin cancers in western nations.

The cost of environmental policies

It is clear that the green case has often been exaggerated. Back in the 1960s, the belief that an increasing world population could not be fed proved false. In the 1970s, the prophecy that the world would soon run out of natural resources turned out to be nonsense. And in recent years, claims about global warming and depletion of the ozone layer have been asserted with more confidence than is justified by the evidence and have been larded with grossly inflated projections of impending doom and disaster.

Nevertheless, is it not wise to err on the side of caution? Is it not sensible to conserve and recycle natural raw materials even if there are enough metals in the top mile of the Earth's crust to last for 100 million years?[27] Is it not prudent to limit carbon emissions even though we do not know that the build-up of carbon dioxide will lead to significant global warming? Is it not a good idea to try to limit population growth in Third World countries even if we can feed more people, or to ban production of CFCs even if fluctuations in the ozone layer may have little or nothing to do with them? Should we not be using the power of governments, whenever we can, to limit the risks to which economic and technological development inevitably exposes us? Is it not better to be on the safe side?

There are a number of problems with this sort of response. One is that every new ban or regulation imposes a cost.[28] Fitting scrubbers to power station chimneys to combat acid rain raises the cost of generating electricity, just as banning CFCs raises the cost of refrigerating medicines in African hospitals. Environmentalists often argue that if environmental assets such as clean rain or a thick ozone layer were properly costed, policies like these could prove to be beneficial rather than damaging to the wealth of a nation. This is an important argument, and, as we shall see later, it may indeed be possible to find a way of pricing environmental goods so that their benefits are properly weighed when decisions come to be made. The basic point remains, however, that when governments decide to ban, restrict or impose conditions upon economic activity, their policies are not costless. Environmental policy always involves trade-offs, or what economists call 'opportunity costs'. Every pound spent on smoke-scrubbing is a pound lost to some other potentially beneficial activity, and it is not necessarily the case that the money is always best spent on the environmental option.[29]

Not only is environmental regulation costly, but the costs often fall upon those least able to afford them. We have already seen how a ban on CFC manufacture hits developing countries particularly hard, but this is not the only example. When American greens managed to secure a ban on the manufacture of Dieldrin on the grounds that it polluted the environment, they succeeded in depriving African farmers of access to the one effective chemical spray which could deal with swarms of locusts.[30] When greens block the construction of dams in undeveloped parts of Third World countries, they succeed in depriving local people of access to electricity and thereby stalling any possibility of raising their standard of living. And when greens succeed in influencing governments to impose limits on carbon emissions, their actions inevitably hinder the development of heavy industry in Third World countries and therefore undermine the ability of these countries to compete more effectively with the West and to raise the living standards of their people.

Environmental policies may also involve costs for future generations. This may appear an odd argument given that greens normally suggest that their policies are designed to protect rather than harm generations yet to be born. The Brundtland Commission's aim of sustainable development, for example, seeks to ensure that each generation does not leave the world in a more impoverished state than when it entered it, and this is taken to mean that we should not use up finite resources but should instead reduce our demands upon the natural environment.

On reflection, however, it seems that industrial capitalism often achieves precisely what the authors of the Brundtland Report claim to want, for there has been no generation in the last 200 years which has not passed on a heritage richer than the one it inherited. This has been achieved precisely by exploiting natural resources and using them to create wealth.[31] It is through economic and technological development that capitalist countries have discovered resources which earlier generations did not know existed, have found alternatives for resources for which earlier generations had no substitutes, and have developed more efficient ways of using resources which earlier generations squandered.

Consider, for example, the invention of the steam engine which, as we saw in Chapter 1, sparked the industrial revolution. When it was invented, coal supplies were limited by the inability to drain water from deep-lying seams. Its invention solved this problem (by enabling water to be pumped from mines) and at the same time led to an expanded demand for coal as steam engines were harnessed to cotton spinning, rail transport and other innovative uses. Had greens been around at the time, they would doubtless have warned that the widespread adoption of this new technology would rapidly exhaust coal supplies to the detriment of later generations. Indeed, in 1865 the economist, Stanley Jevons, issued just such a warning. In his view, industrialization was doomed owing to the shortage of coal needed to fuel the anticipated increase of production in the years to come, and he predicted an increase in the demand for coal from 80 million tons in 1865 to an 'unsustainable' 2600 million tons by 1960.

However, what actually happened was, first, that the increased demand for coal made it increasingly attractive to invest in mining so that more fields were brought into production; second, that steam engines became more efficient so that as time went on they used less coal to produce more energy; and third, that the increased demand for energy produced a strong economic motive for entrepreneurs and explorers to discover alternative means for powering machinery (notably electricity and oil). Jevons's gloomy prophecy was wildly inaccurate. Today Britain consumes only 120 million tons of coal each year (less than 5 per cent of his prediction) and the country's total energy consumption expressed in coal equivalent works out at only 340 million tons.[32]

A technological fix?

In a capitalist market society, if demand for something rises and the supply begins to dwindle, this shows up in increased prices. These increased prices then induce businesses to raise production (e.g. in the case of energy by bringing coal, oil or gas fields on stream which were previously 'uneconomic'), to improve efficiency (e.g. by building lean-burn machines and improving insulation) and to search for substitutes. The market system thus contains its own feedback mechanisms. It is, indeed, much like an ecological system, for both involve perpetual adaptation to changing circumstances which is accomplished unconsciously without overall direction or control from above.

As a result of 200 years of industrialization, the world is richer in resources now than it has ever been. Furthermore, the development of new technologies (e.g. biotechnology, lasers and computer-based applications) means that modern industries often require fewer raw materials than in the past (fibre-optic cables and satellite communications, for example, have dramatically reduced our reliance on copper), they use materials which are in more plentiful supply (the raw material for computer chips, silicon, is found in sand which is effectively limitless in supply), and they create less pollution (the more prosperous capitalist countries become, the more 'environmentally friendly' their industries).

One major reason why so many gloomy green predictions in the past have not been realized is that growth and technological innovation have managed to solve the problems. Despite this, however, many greens remain deeply sceptical about any search for a 'technological fix' for the problems which confront us today, and they prefer instead to go down the route of political imposition or voluntary adoption of austerity programmes. Again, their principal objection concerns the risk factor, for they argue that the discovery of technical solutions in the past does not *guarantee* that appropriate solutions will also be found in the future.[33]

All human activity necessarily entails risk, for we can never be certain of outcomes. The green response to this uncertainty is to argue that we must insure against the worst outcome. Perhaps global warming is not occurring, but if it is, it is going to lead to serious consequences. Perhaps CFCs are not destroying the ozone layer, but if they are then we are all going to suffer in the future. Perhaps new technology can find solutions to many of the problems of continued global population expansion, but if it cannot then the implications of current growth rates look catastrophic. Better, then, to act on these problems now, while there is still time, than to wait until it is too late. As one green commentator puts it:

> We must be given good reason to think that solutions to each and all of the serious problems ahead will be found. Would it not be much wiser and safer to undertake social change to values and structures that do not generate any of these problems?[34]

There are three major objections to this kind of argument. The first is that it sets an impossible hurdle for industrial capitalism to jump over, for we cannot know in advance of its development what technology may become available to us in the future. All that can be said is that the catastrophes predicted by greens in the past have hitherto been avoided by technological developments, that capitalism contains within it an inherent spur to innovation, and that promising research is in progress today on all the problems which threaten danger in the future.[35]

The second objection is that if we allow the minimization of risk to become our overriding concern, then innovation, exploration and experimentation which could benefit future generations will all suffer. It is a unique feature of the so-called 'postmodern' period in which we are living that ours is the first generation seriously to consider whether we should try to stop economic and technological development in its tracks. It is by no means obvious that future generations will look back and thank us for such failings of nerve, any more than we would be grateful had our forebears decided not to open up coal mines or to travel in search of foreign lands. It is arguably no less irresponsible to abandon the pursuit of economic development than to allow it a free reign. So what makes us so sure that now is the time to relinquish the baton and give up the race?

The third objection is perhaps the most serious of all. Much deep green thinking seems simply to assume that a fundamental change of 'values and structures' can be engineered with few problems. All we have to do to avoid our current environmental problems is change society from top to bottom! This not only begs the question of how such a change is to occur and what kind of society will emerge as a result of it, but also betrays a frightening *naïveté* about the ease with which this new Utopia will overcome our problems.[36] Like radical socialists before them, radical greens today wish to drag us kicking and screaming into the Garden of Eden, but we are rarely given a glimpse of what lies on the other side of the fence.

Dismantling capitalism

Left to itself, capitalism clearly cannot resolve all the environmental problems which it creates. Problems of resource depletion can often be resolved through the market mechanism of rising prices, and provided there is money to be made, new technologies can often be relied upon to clean up the mess left by old ones. But what of the other problems identified by green critics? How can capitalist systems deal with environmental problems when there is no price stimulus inducing innovation and no obvious possibility for entrepreneurs to make profit?

Many environmental problems seem to demand governmental or even intergovernmental action if they are to be tackled, for capitalist enterprises seem unwilling or unable to sort out the problems themselves. As many economists have come to recognize, not everything can be left to the market.

In 1833, William Forster Lloyd wrote a pamphlet on the problem of over-exploitation of the common land in English villages prior to the enclosures. His argument was that when pasture land is made available to all, it will be in the interests of each herder to graze as many cattle as possible upon it. This is because the benefit to the individual herder of grazing one extra animal on the free pasture massively outweighs the cost in terms of the slight decline in quality of pasture which is then available for all the animals. But this same logic applies also to every other cattle owner, with the result that the pasture is rapidly exhausted and they all end up with nothing. Even if they recognize the dangers, the herders will not refrain from their damaging behaviour, for if one reduces the number of animals he or she grazes on the land, the benefit will simply be appropriated by others who do not follow suit (game theorists refer to this as the 'free-rider problem'). As Hardin explains in his discussion of Lloyd's original insight: 'Each man is locked into a system that compels him to increase his herd without limit – in a world that is limited. Ruin is the destination toward which all men rush'.[37]

Many of today's environmental problems exhibit the same features as this original 'tragedy of the commons'. Because the oceans are open to all, fishing fleets have every incentive to expand their catches to the point where fish stocks become exhausted and all fleets have to spend longer and longer catching fewer and fewer fish. Similarly, because access to the atmosphere is unlimited, it pays industries to expel waste untreated into the air even though we might all prefer a less polluted atmosphere. Where roads are provided free of charge, they too become part of the 'commons' and individual motorists pursue their own rational self-interest by seeking the convenience of driving everywhere even though they end up in nose-to-tail traffic jams because all the other motorists have followed the same option. And so on.

The tragedy of the commons poses a major problem for market-based capitalism, for it seems that competitive profit-seeking individuals will inevitably exploit the planet to the point of destruction unless the state steps in to stop them. This leads many greens to argue that the tragedy can only be resolved or averted by means of dramatic political solutions.[38] Even the relatively modest Brundtland Report called for 'decisive political action now . . . to ensure . . . human survival',[39] and for many greens, this is too mild in tone and too accommodating in content. Dismissive of such 'reformist thinking', they call for 'breathtakingly radical action' and do not shrink from mounting 'a radical, visionary and fundamentalist challenge to the prevailing economic and political world order'.[40] Capitalism, in short, must be put to the sword.

This radical green agenda is implacably opposed to capitalism, and it is this which brings it close to more traditional socialist positions. Responding to socialist criticisms that they should identify capitalism rather than industrialism as the root cause of environmental problems, one radical green retorts: 'Greens will accept that the destruction of capitalism is indeed a necessary condition for restoring environmental integrity . . . The deeper green programme constitutes a serious threat to both the social relations and productive practices typical of capitalism'.[41] Like revolutionary socialism, deep green environmentalism offers an apocalyptic vision of the future which can only be avoided by wholesale destruction of the present social order and its replacement with a new one. Also, like revolutionary socialism, its adherents seem often to teeter on the brink of totalitarian political solutions and, as in the example of their dramatic prescriptions for population control, sometimes to topple over into them. More often, however, they avoid confronting the political implications of their programme, but it is difficult to see how radical changes designed to withdraw the comforts of modern consumerism and to plunge us all into bleak austerity could be achieved without resort to considerable force.

Although it shares much in common with old-style socialism, however, the radical green movement is more than simply socialism in a new guise. Environmentalists themselves generally claim that they are neither on the left nor the right, that they are 'neither red nor blue but green'. They are anti-capitalist, but they are also in one important sense anti-socialist, for they see both systems as contaminated by a faith in and reliance upon technological progress and economic growth. Most greens are well aware of the ecological disaster which was unleashed in Russia and eastern Europe under socialism and which only finally came to light after the 1989 revolutions,[42] and they know that nowhere in the western capitalist nations is there evidence of environmental degradation of the scale or intensity which occurred throughout the eastern European socialist regimes.

Green capitalism: commodifying the environment

The deep green answer to the tragedy of the commons seems inevitably to end up in political coercion – we must be stopped from overpopulating the planet, from using up resources, from pumping carbon dioxide into the atmosphere, and so on. But there is an alternative green vision, for the need to find an answer to the tragedy of the commons need not always entail increased direction by public authorities.

The starting point for this alternative approach lies in the recognition that, if markets sometimes fail, so too do governments. Motivated by the best of intentions, government agencies often exacerbate the problems which they intend to resolve, for they can never have at their disposal all the information needed to work out all the implications of pursuing a particular course of action. This suggests that government controls should be tried only when market-based solutions have proved inadequate.

Consider as an example the problems of protecting endangered species of wildlife. In Kenya, the government responded to environmentalists' concerns about the declining number of elephants by agreeing to impose a ban on ivory trading. This, however, simply raised the black market price of ivory and therefore increased the incentives for poachers to kill even more elephants. In Zimbabwe, by contrast, the government introduced a licensing system for ivory trading under which revenue from tusks and from hunting permits went back to local communities who therefore had an interest in policing poaching themselves. Elephant numbers have been rising by 5 per cent per year as a result.[43]

The lesson to be drawn from this is that it is not capitalist trade, but the absence of clearly defined property rights, which results in overexploitation of natural resources. When resources have a market value and can be bought and sold as private property, they tend not to disappear, for owners then have an interest in maintaining and reproducing them. It is this that explains why the free-roaming American buffalo was wiped out while cows graze on the same land today in their thousands, or why crocodiles (which governments allow to be farmed for their skins) are in plentiful supply while rhinoceroses (which roam free in reserves and are poached for their horns) are on the endangered species list.[44] Seen in this light, the tragedy of the commons has less to do with the absence of government regulation on how the commons may be used than with the absence of any identifiable proprietorial interest in them.

There are three ways in which the capitalist profit motive may be harnessed to produce environmentally beneficial results. One is by means of 'green consumerism', for if there is an effective demand for products which do not damage the environment, capitalist producers will begin to compete to supply it. The second is by introducing charges for access to common resources which have hitherto been available free or at subsidized prices, for this builds the cost of resource depletion or despoliation into the economic calculations of those who use them. The third and most radical is by privatizing or commodifying public goods.

The growth of public awareness of green issues has led in recent years to a new market in environmentally friendly products in Europe and North America. Big industrial firms such as ICI and Shell have spent millions of pounds on environmental programmes and advertise their concern on national television. Car companies compete with each other to produce clean, energy-efficient models which can be recycled at the end of their useful lives. Financial institutions profitably specialize in 'ethical investments' which avoid companies which pollute the planet. Supermarkets now sell organic foodstuffs free of contaminating chemicals, eggs produced by free-range chickens and toilet tissue manufactured from recycled paper. Manufacturers of washing powders market low-phosphorus products which will not choke the rivers with foaming suds, and even before the ban on CFCs aerosol manufacturers were rushing to market products guaranteed not to damage the ozone layer. And retailers such as Body Shop have achieved remarkable success throughout the western world by concentrating on product lines which they claim are not tested on animals, which are purchased at a 'fair price' from Third World producers, and which do not damage the natural environment.

All of this activity is proving very profitable. Having founded her first Body Shop in 1976, for example, Anita Roddick is now worth over £100 million and was listed by *The Sunday Times* in 1994 as the 106th richest individual in Britain.

Green consumerism by itself is, however, unlikely to be sufficient to meet all the problems and challenges, and capitalist market solutions to environmental problems must go beyond simply leaving green-minded consumers to demand environmentally sound products. Even if millions of us insist on buying liquids in glass bottles rather than plastic containers, this will not solve the problem of disposing of waste, and it is difficult to see how changes in purchasing decisions by individual consumers could help sort out problems such as the possible danger of global warming. Green capitalism will often require some degree of government action in order to enable market-based solutions to develop.

One form of government action which uses the market to bring about desired environmental objectives is the introduction of new pricing policies. An obvious example is the lower duty levied by many western governments on unleaded than on leaded petrol. This has served as an effective inducement to motorists to switch their purchasing patterns (and for car manufacturers to change their engine requirements) without the need for political controls or bans.

The point about a policy like this is that, unlike blanket government regulation, it leaves it up to individual users to decide how best to adapt their behaviour. Drivers who can switch relatively easily to unleaded fuel have done so; those who cannot must now pay a premium which expresses the fact that their behaviour is generating a social cost (i.e. that they are polluting the commons).

It has been suggested that in practice there may turn out to be little difference between government pricing strategies and the use of political directives and bans to achieve the same result.[45] The crucial difference, however, is that political regulation imposes uniform standards on everybody in order to meet a specified target, whereas pricing strategies tend to bring about the biggest shift in behaviour among those for whom change is least costly. Not only is this latter strategy more sensitive to individual liberties, but it will also prove a more efficient way of achieving the desired aggregate result.

The introduction of charges has often proved effective as a means of pollution control in situations where polluting activities were previously a cost-free option. In England, for example, the discharge of farm and industrial waste into the river system had for years been controlled by a simple licensing system in which farmers and industrialists applied for 'discharge consents' which allowed them to pump a certain volume of waste into a specified river or stream. The problem with this system was that there was no incentive to reduce the volume or toxicity of discharge. Recognizing this, the National Rivers Authority has now introduced a new system in which those seeking to discharge waste into the rivers must pay for the right to do so. The more waste they pump out, the higher the price they must pay, and this helps meet the cost of cleaning up the rivers.[46]

This 'polluter pays' system does not seek to eradicate pollution altogether (for the rivers can handle a certain level of discharge and there is no other feasible way of disposing of large volumes of liquid waste), but it does ensure that the 'marginal external costs' of individuals' actions are properly taken into account when they decide between different courses of action. As with the example of lead-free petrol, those who can easily cut back on their polluting activities will find that it pays them to do so, while those who cannot will have to accept the higher charges which their activities incur.

The polluter pays principle is successfully being applied in many areas of environmental concern. In some German towns, for example, garbage trucks are now fitted with meters which weigh domestic refuse and automatically bill households according to the amount of waste they throw out. This system both encourages households to reduce waste and raises the revenue required to dispose of it. A similar strategy is being applied on a larger scale with the introduction by governments throughout Europe of carbon taxes as the means for tackling the (perceived) problem of global warming. Here again, consumers are encouraged to reduce emission of waste (in this case CO_2 emissions from coal-burning power stations) by raising the price they must pay for their electricity.

In California, this principle of charging for pollution has been taken one step further with the establishment of a market in tradable pollution permits.[47] In 1994, a Regional Clean Air Incentives Market was established across four counties in southern California to allocate pollution credits among 390 companies which between them produce most of the industrial pollution in the area. Each credit allows a company to discharge 2.2 kilograms of nitrogen oxides or sulphur oxides, and each company was given a limit on its total emissions. Those which manage to stay below their limit will be able to sell their surplus credits at auction to those who continue to exceed theirs. As overall emission limits are progressively reduced by the government, so the price of traded credits will rise. It is expected that overall emissions of nitrogen oxides and sulphur oxides will fall by 75 per cent and 60 per cent, respectively, over a ten-year period.

Policies like tradable pollution permits take us into the third way of pursuing environmental benefits through capitalist market strategies, for what the Californian experiment has effectively done is to commodify the right of factory owners to use the air which was previously 'provided' to them free. As we saw in Chapter 1, for capitalism to function it is necessary for government to establish and enforce a clear system of private property rights. In many instances of environmental pollution and neglect, this is precisely what has been missing. Nobody owns the rainforest, or the ozone layer, or the North Sea, which is why everybody feels free to abuse them. Tradable pollution permits represent a particularly elegant market solution to the tragedy of the commons in the air, but this same market logic can also be applied in water.

In Australia, for example, overfishing of tuna was a problem because the ocean was a free resource for anybody with a boat and a net. Rather than trying to conserve fish stocks, as many European governments have done, by keeping boats in port for a specified number of days each month or by regulating the length of nets, the Australian government introduced tradable fishing quotas. Fishing boats are allocated a maximum quota, and these quotas can then be traded. The result is that the most efficient crews tend to buy up extra quotas from the least efficient. Environmental standards (in this case, fish stocks) are maintained, but not at the cost of economic efficiency.[48]

Of course, not all environmental problems are susceptible to market-based solutions like this, for it is not always possible clearly to specify the boundaries of a property holding, in which case common holdings cannot easily be privatized. Territory on land can usually be marked out and fenced in, and we have seen that rights over water and local air space may also be established and defended, but such solutions can become extremely difficult when applied to property rights in the atmosphere. Some important environmental resources, including the ozone layer and the stability of the global climate, cannot easily be privatized and therefore may not readily lend themselves to a capitalist market solution.

However, given a little political wisdom and the appropriate technology, property rights in the environment could be extended much further than they are at present. Just as the invention of barbed wire in the 1840s helped solve the overexploitation of the American prairies by enabling claimants to fence their land, so too modern technological developments could similarly help resolve some of today's environmental problems by enabling individuals to establish and defend clear property rights in the atmosphere against the claims or abuses of others.[49]

For example, chemical tracers could be added to emissions from chimneys which would allow those who suffer from atmospheric pollution from factories to charge those who are responsible for it. This would mean that owners of Scandinavian lakes could seek compensation from owners of power stations in England for the acidification of their water rights and the death of their fish. The owners of the power stations would then either pass on these external costs in the prices they charged for their electricity, or would invest in chimney-scrubbers in order to reduce the amount of compensation they had to pay. Either way, the value of the environment, which is currently ignored in the accounts, would properly be recognized and would enter into people's behaviour.

Road pricing is another way of cutting down pollution. Several western governments seem likely to move soon to a computerized system for monitoring car use in cities and billing drivers on a monthly basis, but the principle could be extended by privatizing the highways and charging the firms which run them for the pollution which their customers are generating. Such charges would presumably be passed on to road users, with higher tolls at peak periods when exhaust emissions are at their worst, and this would in turn lead drivers to amend their behaviour (e.g. by travelling off-peak, by car pooling, or by switching to alternative modes of transport) by taking account of pollution costs which are currently socialized.

Taken to the extremes of technical and practical feasibility, we could even imagine a property rights solution to problems such as the decline in the whale population. It has been reported that Americans would on average be prepared to pay $8 each to prevent the extinction of the blue whale.[50] These creatures therefore have a value to people but there is no way at present that this can be translated into effective purchasing power. Rather than leaving them at the mercy of hunters for whom they represent a free good, it might make sense to sell particular whales to interested parties (such as individual Americans or members of Greenpeace), 'brand' them by genetic prints, and monitor them by satellite. In such a futuristic scenario, the plight of the world's whales could be relieved by the establishment of effective private ownership so that whaling fleets would have to pay market rates in compensation if they continued to catch creatures which would no longer be freely available to any who wished to go out with a harpoon gun.

Market capitalism and environmental quality are not inherently incompatible. It is all too easy to be seduced by the claim that big environmental problems demand draconian political solutions. Not all of the world's environmental problems can be resolved by pricing and privatizing resources, nor might we find technological solutions in every case, but lasting solutions are more likely to be found by governments working with the grain of individual self-interest as revealed in market behaviour, rather than against it. Some of the problems identified by the green movement are real, and they demand a response, but this does not mean that the time has come to turn off the capitalist growth machine. The growth of capitalist economies will continue to cause environmental problems, but continuing economic growth and technical innovation within a context of market relations and private property rights arguably offers our best hope for overcoming them. The deep green alternative of bleak austerity necessarily enforced through political coercion is not one which the world need, or is willing to, accept.

Capitalism and Human Happiness

We have seen in preceeding chapters how, economically and technically, capitalism has proved itself. Not only can it provide us with video recorders and the technological wizardry of virtual reality, but it can also feed the world and perhaps even save the whale.

The really big question, however, is whether the output of the capitalist growth machine over the last two hundred years has made human beings any happier. We are all familiar with the observations of older people who wistfully report that they were poorer yet happier in days gone by, and we all know the homespun truths that 'money cannot buy happiness' and that human beings 'cannot live by bread alone'. Clearly, then, a social audit of contemporary capitalism needs to consider the question of whether the quality of people's lives has really been improved by the expansion of output which this system has brought about. Are we any happier now that we have our cars, our foreign holidays, our double glazing and our home-delivery pizzas?

The pursuit of happiness

Social systems cannot make people happy. All that any set of social institutions can reasonably be expected to do is to provide the conditions in which individuals can pursue happiness.

In the 1940s the psychologist, Abraham Maslow, identified a 'hierarchy' of human needs.[1] The most basic and fundamental needs were those deriving from the physiological requirements of the human organism – the need for food and shelter, for example. If these needs were not satisfied, then, according to Maslow, their absence would eclipse all other concerns, but once they were met, individuals would become aware of further needs. These included the need for safety, the need for intimacy and a sense of belonging, the need for self-esteem and respect, and, finally, the need for self-actualization, the fulfilment of one's potential.

Reviewing Maslow's work, Charles Murray finds in it a concise summary of the conditions necessary for human beings to find happiness.[2] If individuals are unable to achieve access to adequate food and shelter, or find themselves threatened with physical harm, or are deprived of intimacy, or are denied the recognition and self-respect warranted by their behaviour, or are blocked in their attempts to fulfil their full potential, then we may suggest that social conditions are to blame for inhibiting the possibility of human happiness. Equally, as Murray suggests, if all five of Maslow's needs are met, then it is difficult to suggest that an individual has been prevented by external conditions from pursuing or achieving happiness. There is only so much that a social system can be expected to do; the rest we must do for ourselves.

How, then, does capitalism measure up on these five criteria? According to Karl Marx, it performs miserably. We saw in Chapter 1 how Marx believed that capitalism falls at Maslow's first hurdle, for his 'immiseration thesis' held that the mass of the population would become materially worse off the more capitalism developed. In Marx's view, a capitalist system cannot even provide for the most basic of human needs.

Marx was also convinced that capitalism could not provide the other conditions of human happiness identified a century later in Maslow's hierarchy. In his analysis of 'alienation', he suggested that the human need for intimacy and belonging was subverted under capitalism by what he called 'the estrangement of man from man',[3] for in capitalist societies people relate to each other in their economic roles as workers or as capitalists, rather than in terms of their intrinsic qualities as human beings. Workers, for example, are depersonalized by a system of wage labour which treats them simply as muscle or brain power which can be used to create commodities, rather than as fully rounded people.

Alienation under capitalism was also revealed in people's inability to fulfil their need for self-actualization. Workers under capitalism were aliented both from the product of their labour (which is taken away from them as soon as it is created), and from the act of labour (which is 'shunned like the plague' once the compulsion to work is lifted).[4] Capitalism thus distorts what it is to be human and subverts our need as a species to express ourselves through our labour. Work, which should be our central life activity, has become merely a means to an end. We exercise no control over it, and we take no joy in it.

We have seen that Marx's immiseration thesis has turned out to be a nonsense, but these other aspects of his critique of capitalism are less easily dismissed. There is indeed more to life than material prosperity, and there are signs that capitalism's success in meeting people's material needs may not of itself have made them any more contented.

Material needs: money cannot buy happiness

The growing affluence of capitalist countries led some of those who followed Marx in the twentieth century to abandon his economic critique of capitalism and to focus instead on his theory of alienation. Probably the best known of these writers was Herbert Marcuse, who sought to blend Marx's humanistic concerns about alienation with Sigmund Freud's ideas about the subconscious sublimation of instinctive needs and desires.[5]

According to Marcuse, modern capitalism stimulates 'false needs' for ever more material goods. These needs are awakened in us by corporations which lure us with the glitter of the commodities they produce, and they are constantly renewed by the advertising industry and mass culture. By striving to satisfy these false needs, we lock ourselves into our own continued repression, for we learn to demand of capitalism the one thing which it can supply; namely, more goods. Meanwhile, our 'real needs', expressing our basic instincts (and in particular our libido), are 'repressively desublimated' in a one-dimensional world of commodities. The sex drive and other instinctual needs are channelled into forms of expression which are ultimately unsatisfying. Mass culture with its Hollywood tinsel films and its pulp romantic novels, and mass consumption with its glitzy advertising and its unrealizable promises of satisfaction through possession of things, offer us forms of release and expression which are containable and controllable within the existing social system, yet which are always unfulfilling for the individuals who live in it. All the libidinal energy of the mass of the population is therefore used up in ways that do not threaten the system, and for as long as capitalism can continue to produce new commodities, it can successfully continue to control people. Technical progress defuses all opposition.

There is much that is questionable in Marcuse's critique of contemporary capitalism, not least his assertion that he can identify as 'false' those needs which 'the masses' seem uncritically to accept as 'real'. For all its problems, however, Marcuse's essay does alert us to a real problem, for the search for happiness and contentment through the pursuit of material goods seems inherently elusive in modern capitalist societies. The more we get, the less satisfied we seem to be. In a world of bountiful commodities, we seem to be locked into a spiral of ever increasing accumulation as we seek to attain an always elusive sense of final contentment. Like a heroin addict, we need more and more stimulus to achieve the same level of 'high'.

Why is it that under modern capitalism our demands appear to be limitless and insatiable? Is capitalism itself in some way responsible for this poignant feature of the contemporary consumer experience?

In one sense it seems that it is. In capitalist market economies, individuals seek 'utility' through purchase of goods and services, but in many cases the utility they are able to derive from their purchases declines when other individuals buy the same goods. The purchase of a car, for example, holds the promise of enhanced personal freedom and mobility, but if everybody has a car the roads soon become congested and the satisfaction gained by each user is correspondingly diminished. Similarly, pursuit of qualifications such as a university degree can only lead to a better job with high pay for as long as few other people are able to gain such qualifications, for once degrees become commonplace, competition among graduates for highly remunerated positions is intensified.

The problem faced by individuals in competition for such 'positional goods' is akin to having to walk up a down escalator which is travelling ever faster. Precisely because capitalism increases the general level of prosperity, more and more people are able to gain access to desired goods and the satisfaction to be gained from possession of the goods is in consequence reduced. Competition for relative advantage becomes increasingly intensified while individuals experience mounting frustration and disappointment when they discover that the items to which they have aspired fail to deliver the advantages they had expected. As Hirsch explains: 'The distributional struggle returns, heightened rather than relieved by the dynamic process of growth. It is an exact reversal of what economists and present-day politicians have come to expect growth to deliver'.[6] According to Hirsch, the only way out of this bind is for individuals to seek real improvements in their common welfare by means of collective cooperation and a redistribution of resources between them.

Not all goods, however, are positional goods, and in many cases the potential satisfaction to be gained from consumption of a particular commodity does not depend upon others being denied access to it. My enjoyment of my foreign holiday may be marred by the fact that hordes of other tourists can also descend upon the same location at the same time, but there are many areas of personal consumption where pleasure can be derived irrespective of how many other people make similar purchases. Clearly Hirsch's analysis cannot be the full story, for we have still to ask why our consumption of non-positional goods is so often characterized by a lack of ultimate fulfilment and the perpetual search for more.

One hundred years ago, Emile Durkheim attributed this 'malady of infinite aspiration' to rapid and disruptive economic and technological change. Durkheim believed that human wants are in principle limitless, and he understood that individuals who are slaves to their own unlimited desires can never be satisfied and can never achieve happiness. Unless our desires and demands are somehow held in check, it therefore follows that we must be condemned for ever to chase an unattainable end. This, said Durkheim, is a recipe for unhappy individuals and a morbid society: 'To pursue a goal which is by definition unattainable is to condemn oneself to a state of perpetual unhappiness . . . The more one has, the more one wants, since satisfactions received only stimulate instead of filling needs'.[7]

In Durkheim's view, human 'passions' can only be held in check by the moral force of society. In other words, individuals need to learn and understand the limits to which they may realistically aspire. In preindustrial times, this was easily accomplished, for social change was slow and the social order seemed almost immutable. We 'knew' from an early age the life to which we were ordained, and in feudal Europe these norms were reinforced by the power of the law and the majesty of religion. Today, by contrast, the capitalist growth machine is for ever speeding up, and this perpetually revolutionizes our expectations and aspirations. The limited horizons of our forebears have been blown apart, for the pace of change is such that new norms and new patterns of expectation have no time to settle before they too are superseded. We do not know what we can demand or expect out of life, for the norms by which we live are in constant flux. In Durkheim's terms, there is in modern societies a pathology of normative deregulation, or 'anomie', which generates personal unhappiness and social disorder.

Durkheim's solution to this lay in the development of a more ordered form of capitalism. Capitalism required regulation, not by governments (for Durkheim was clear that the state is too remote from people's everyday lives to exert moral influence over them), but through new forms of voluntary association based upon the workplace. Although he did not develop these ideas to any great extent, the forms of corporate loyalty and responsibility found today in countries such as Japan and Germany seem broadly consistent with the sort of institutional developments he had in mind. We consider this so-called 'Rhine model' of capitalism in Chapter 5.

Rapid economic and technological change cannot, however, fully explain our seemingly limitless desire for material goods. It is not just the pace of change since the start of the industrial revolution, but also the cultural transformation which occurred in Europe prior to industrialization, which has produced our modern patterns of consumerism.

In a stimulating study of this cultural transformation, Colin Campbell contrasts the apparently limitless desires of modern consumers with traditional patterns of consumption in which wants were relatively fixed.[8] Drawing a direct parallel with Weber's analysis of the origins of the capitalist ethic, Campbell argues that a cultural shift must have occurred in the West which led people to expand their limited desires and to embrace a new ethic which emphasized the pleasure to be gained from the never ending pursuit of goods. Indeed, the development of modern capitalism depended not only upon a revolution in traditional patterns of working (something achieved by the impact of Protestantism), but also upon a corresponding shift in traditional modes of consuming, for a new consumption ethic was required to create the markets for the goods being produced by the new capitalist enterprises.

Just as Weber saw Puritanism as the source of the capitalist work ethic, so Campbell sees Puritanism also as the unwitting source of this new consumer ethic. Puritanism was, of course, opposed to all forms of hedonism and emotional display, but by training people to control their emotions it fostered a division between inner feelings and outward actions. People learned to derive emotional pleasure from inner contemplation entirely divorced from external physical stimuli, and this gradually enabled them to seek emotional gratification entirely within the imagination.

As the significance of religion declined, so this search for emotional gratification was displaced into romanticism and sentimentality. People learned to fantasize and to daydream, and the eighteenth-century novel catered handsomely to these appetites. The legacy of this romanticism today is that we still seek and derive emotional pleasure within the imagination through the anticipation of future gratification. The enjoyment is much more in the anticipation than in the consummation of consumption. We take pleasure in planning our next holiday even as we return from the last one, in poring over the catalogues more than in taking delivery of the goods, in window-shopping for new clothes as opposed to wearing them in the weeks and months following the purchase. In our romantic imaginations, the items we desire are always perfect, but the reality of subsequent experience always falls short of such flawlessness so that the pleasure of possession swiftly palls. Wants and desires are thus perpetually renewed as we find intense inner pleasure in the anticipation of the next purchase.

If Campbell is right, it means not only that capitalism did not create the modern malaise of infinite aspiration, but also that the transcendence of capitalism would be unlikely to resolve it. Having let the genie of our imaginations out of the bottle, it cannot easily be put back in again.

The need for security and intimacy

Once some basic level of material need has been met, further consumption is unlikely to add very much to human happiness and other needs will therefore come into focus. In particular, we require a certain minimum level of safety and personal security and we are likely to feel a need for intimacy and a sense of belonging. As we shall see, these two are related.

There is a long tradition of thought in western sociology which holds that capitalism has destroyed the basis for intimacy and belonging in social life. One of the key sources of this belief lies in the late nineteenth-century work of Ferdinand Tönnies. Tönnies set out to explore the 'sentiments and motives which draw people to each other, keep them together, and induce them to joint action'.[9] His basic thesis was that the expansion of trade and the subsequent development of industrial capitalism had weakened relationships based upon what he called 'natural will' (i.e. feelings and instincts), and had substituted relations grounded in 'rational will' (i.e. instrumental calculation). More specifically, he believed that natural sentiments which draw people together derive from common kinship (a unity of blood), common neighbourhood (a unity of place) and shared religious faith (a unity of belief). All three had been disrupted in the 'bourgeois' era which put an emphasis on monetary calculation and the narrow pursuit of individual self-interest through market transactions.

Tönnies's analysis has been enormously influential in shaping twentieth-century thinking about modern forms of sociation, yet there are at least three major problems with his argument. First, his analysis of social relations under urban industrial capitalism is one-sided. It emphasizes the negative aspects of modern individualism and neglects its positive features. Second, empirical evidence indicates that Tönnies exaggerated the extent to which intimacy and a sense of personal security have been eroded in contemporary capitalist societies, although recent developments suggest that his prognosis may carry more weight in the twenty-first century than it did for much of the twentieth. And third, the assumption of an inherent link between capitalism and individualism must itself be questioned, for individualism was not born of capitalism, nor do these two always go hand in hand in the contemporary world.

On the first point, it is true that some features of those institutions which traditionally fostered a sense of identity and belonging – family, church and village community – have been weakened as a result of the growth of capitalism, for the unprecedented rate of industrial and technical change over the last two hundred years has been associated with massive disruption of traditional society. As we saw in Chapter 1, agricultural workers in England were pushed off the land by enclosures and were lured or obliged to move to the new cities in search of employment, and this pattern of mass rural–urban migration within or across national borders has subsequently been repeated in many other parts of the world touched by industrial capitalism.

It is also true that modern capitalism creates conditions of insecurity at the same time as it disrupts old social arrangements. In most of western Europe and the United States, unemployment now seems endemic, and young people can experience real difficulties in finding secure work. In Britain, for example, between 1981 and 1992 the unemployment rate fluctuated between 6.8 per cent and 12.4 per cent, and in 1993 22 per cent of 'economically active' male teenagers and 16 per cent of 'economically active' female teenagers were unemployed (in the United States, the unemployment rate has been slightly lower during this period, varying between 5.2 per cent and 9.5 per cent).[10] The possibility of redundancy and the problems faced by some young people in finding work create a fear of economic insecurity despite continued rises in average real incomes and the availability of state welfare support for those who cannot support themselves. Research in North America on each of Maslow's five needs found that people were more troubled by lack of financial security than by any other single item.[11]

Nor are feelings of insecurity limited to problems of unemployment and redundancy. The experience of perpetual change in the modern world is almost certainly incompatible with any strong sense of enduring order or a stable sense of belonging, for it disrupts settled patterns of sociability. Where once our lives were grounded in familiar routines based upon the centrality of kinship and ties to natal localities, we are today forced to place our trust in strangers with whom we never directly interact.[12] Because modern social life has been 'stretched' over space and time, we are dependent upon the activities of countless numbers of faceless people scattered across the globe rather than upon the actions of those who are physically and emotionally close to us. This means that we are obliged to place our trust in those we do not know, and this fundamental change in the nature of our experience of trust, security, risk and danger places a huge existential question mark at the centre of our everyday lives. The old certainties have disappeared and the future is always to a greater or lesser extent threatening. Ontological security in the modern world is inherently fragile.

But there is another side to all of this. Insecurity is the price we pay for increased personal freedoms. With the erosion of communal ties has come liberation from the perpetual surveillance of family, neighbours and priests. If we are uncertain about where we belong, it is because there are today so many places where we can go, so many different groups with whom we are free to interact, and such a diversity of identities through which we may choose to express different facets of our personalities.[13]

The anonymity of much of modern social life therefore has its benefits. If in large groups the individual stands alone, that individual can also expect to be left alone to lead his or her own life without interference from others. A society where everybody knows everybody else's business may seem cosy, but it is also stifling. Precisely because our lives today are not circumscribed by the tightly drawn concentric circles of family, neighbourhood and church, we are free to engage in a variety of different social circles which may intersect with each other only partially if at all. It is therefore possible for us to devote different aspects of our identities to different areas of our lives and to keep at arm's length those whose intimacy we do not seek.

Even the reliance upon monetary exchanges has its social benefits as well as its social costs. Simmel shows how the medium of money reduces qualitative differences to a standardized, quantitative measure and in this sense levels down the diversity of human experiences since Ford motor cars, Picasso etchings and the sexual favours of prostitutes can all be expressed in terms of a common unit of value. Yet this is also a source of individual freedom and independence. Money may well depersonalize, but it also empowers precisely because a money economy is not interested in the personality of the individual who tenders the credit card or writes the cheque. Money transactions tend to be gender-blind, race-blind and nationality-blind. In a market economy, my money is as good as yours, be I black or white, beautiful or ugly, clever or stupid, noble or of common birth.

The first response to Tönnies, therefore, is that even if intimacy and a sense of belonging have declined as compared with the period before the onset of industrial capitalism, this has enabled individuals to expand the scope of their lives, to explore different facets of their personalities and to develop new faculties and capacities which would in earlier times have remained latent, stifled and unfulfilled.

We can, however, go further than this, for the belief that intimacy and a sense of security have been lost in the transition to modernity has itself to be questioned.

It has long been assumed that close-knit family and community networks were eroded with the onset of industrialization. The 'extended family' (in which parents and their offspring live together with other kin such as grandparents and function as a single economic unit) is thought to have been replaced by the more isolated 'nuclear family' (consisting solely of parents and their immature children). Similarly, the cohesive rural community in which everybody knows everybody else is thought to have been replaced by an 'urban' lifestyle in which relationships are shallow and exploitative. In short, the emotional richness of social relations in the past is said to have been replaced by a colder, more instrumental orientation to life.

This argument almost certainly exaggerates the degree of intimacy in the past, for social historians have demonstrated that extended kinship ties were not as widespread or significant in preindustrial Europe as has generally been believed. In seventeenth-century England, for example, most households were small (fewer than five people), and consisted only of parents and their immature offspring, and fewer than 4 per cent of household members consisted of extended kin.[14] Nor was local community life in preindustrial England as settled and stable as is commonly believed, for Fischer documents rates of residential instability in sixteenth- and seventeenth-century rural England comparable with those of the modern era, and he suggests that rootlessness has been prevalent for at least 12 generations.[15]

Such evidence casts considerable doubt on the view that industrial capitalism broke up extended family ties or smashed the stability of local community networks. Obviously the industrial revolution did spark off a major upheaval in people's lives, but the intimacy and security of the preindustrial world was never as strong as writers like Tönnies seemed to assume.

As Fischer points out, the belief that intimacy has declined rests upon the implicit assumption that a sense of community depends upon ties to a particular place. Following Tönnies, it has too often been assumed that improvements in communications and transportation which enabled people to move more freely between places, and which therefore weakened people's ties to particular localities, led inexorably to a decline in a sense of community. Today, however, many people find that their closest and most meaningful friendships are not with people who live nearby, but are scattered over space. Community has in this sense not disappeared, but has simply been 'stretched' over a wider area. The neighbour- hood has not completely lost its significance for us, of course, but in many cases we now live in territorial communities of limited liability, balancing a civil regard for our neighbours with our own desire for privacy and freedom from constant surveillance. With a greater choice over where we live and the people with whom we interact, the quality of our most intimate relationships is more likely to have been enhanced than diminished.[16]

It is, however, necessary to enter a lengthy caveat at this point, for notwithstanding all the evidence to suggest that our needs for intimacy and security can still be met in the modern period, there are signs that things have, recently, started going wrong.

In most of the western capitalist countries, people's experience of family and community life has been changing dramatically since the 1960s. In Britain, for example, the divorce rate per thousand married people rose from 2.1 in 1961 to 13.4 in 1991 – an increase by a factor in excess of 6 in just 30 years.[17] Marriages are also breaking down more quickly. In 1961 only 1 per cent of divorces occurred within two years of marriage, but by 1991 the figure was 9 per cent. Clearly marriage no longer offers people a realistic prospect of lifetime loyalty with a partner, and this may well have undermined people's ability to establish an enduring emotional bedrock on which to construct the rest of their lives.

The erosion of lifetime marriage affects not only mature adults, but also their children. Illegitimacy rates, like divorce rates, have been rising fast in the last 30 years. Charles Murray[18] shows that throughout the 500 years up to 1950, around 95 per cent of children born in England and Wales were born to married parents. In the late 1950s, however, the illegitimacy rate began to rise, and between 1960 and 1992 it spiralled from 5.2 per cent to 32 per cent. Like the divorce rate, therefore, the illegitimacy rate has increased by a factor of 6 in just 30 years.

It is often suggested that these figures do not necessarily indicate that family life is collapsing, for most divorcees remarry, and many illegitimate children are born to cohabiting parents in stable, long-term relationships. Murray's evidence shows, however, that the success rate of second marriages is even worse than that for first marriages and that cohabiting couples do not even stay together for as long as couples in unsuccessful marriages (the median duration of cohabitations is around two years, as compared with ten years for marriages ending in divorce). Children born to unmarried parents are also much more likely to end up with only one of them, for nearly half of these children are not raised by their father and mother living together in the same household.

Rising divorce rates and the instability of relationships based upon cohabitation have also helped increase the numbers of people living on their own. In 1991, 27 per cent of all households in Britain consisted of individuals living alone – double the proportion recorded just 30 years earlier.

A society in which one marriage in three ends in divorce, in which cohabitation as an alternative to marriage is extremely unstable, in which nearly one child in three is born to parents who choose not to commit themselves to each other by means of marriage, and in which over a quarter of all households consist of people living on their own, looks increasingly like a society in which people are unwilling or unable to make binding and lasting emotional commitments to one another. Even Tönnies would have been amazed by these statistics.

At the same time as family bonds have been weakening, the insecurity posed by the threat of crime has been growing. The total number of criminal offences notified to the police in Britain nearly doubled between 1981 and 1992 to over 5½ million, and violence against the person increased by over 100 per cent during this period[19] (in the United States, violent crimes are even more prevalent than in Britain, though the overall crime rate is lower). Experience as a victim of crime is now commonplace. The 1991 British Crime Survey found that 9 per cent of motorists fall victim to theft from cars every year, and Norman Dennis and George Erdos have calculated that the average citizen is now 47 times more likely to be the victim of crime than was the case immediately before the First World War.[20]

This extraordinary increase in the crime rate is reflected in high levels of fear of crime among the population. In Britain, around one-fifth of the population now say they are 'very worried' about being burgled, and the same proportion express serious fears about being mugged or robbed, or having their car stolen or broken into.

One-third of the population feel unsafe walking in their own neighbourhood after dark (a proportion that rises to 58 per cent among women over 60), and 11 per cent feel very or fairly unsafe in their own homes at night. Among elderly people, 6 per cent never go out alone at night for fear of becoming the victim of crime.[21]

In the United States and in Britain, most crime is committed by young males. In England and Wales in 1991, one in twenty boys had been cautioned or convicted of an indictable offence by the age of 14, and among 18-year-olds this figure exceeded one in ten.[22] This level of criminalization indicates a society in which fundamental norms of civility and social responsibility seem to be fraying badly, particularly in the case of adolescent males. Does this have anything to do with contemporary capitalism?

During the 1980s, right-wing governments in Britain and the United States deliberately sought to stimulate a renewed spirit of individualism and capitalist acquisitiveness. The 1980s witnessed the emergence of a 'yuppie' culture in which money and conspicuous consumption played a key role, and social inequalities widened as a result of rising unemployment and cuts in social welfare. The highest earners in Britain increased their incomes by 62 per cent in real terms between 1979 and 1994, while the poorest tenth of households saw their real incomes fall by 17 per cent.[23]

It seems plausible to link this renewed emphasis on acquisition, coupled with the widening gap between the haves and have-nots, with the spectacular rise in crime and social irresponsibility in these countries. In sociological parlance, all the emphasis was placed on the goal of monetary success while insufficient attention was paid to the normatively approved means for achieving it,[24] and the youths standing in the dole queues responded in predictable fashion. Society cannot function by the market alone, and even some free market liberals have now begun to criticize the Thatcher years for their emphasis on individual acquisitiveness at the expense of moral cohesion.[25] As the rise in criminality in Russia since 1990 demonstrates, capitalism requires a secure moral order if it is not to degenerate into a system in which individuals simply take what they can get and disregard the claims and needs of others.

Crime rates, however, have been rising rapidly in many western capitalist countries, including those governed by social democratic regimes where social inequalities did not widen appreciably through the 1980s. Furthermore, the rising trend in crime in Britain began long before Thatcher came into office, at a time when unemployment was still negligible and the welfare state was well established and was not under threat. Clearly, then, the root causes of the problem cannot be located in the politics of the 1980s.

Norman Dennis and George Erdos have reviewed the crime rate in Britain from 1860 to 1990.[26] They found that the rate remained fairly constant, at or below 1 per cent, throughout this entire period up until the mid-1950s. It then began to climb steeply, to 2 per cent in the early 1960s, 3 per cent by 1970, 5 per cent by 1980, and passing 7 per cent by 1990. In other words, the crime rate began to spiral 20 years or more before Margaret Thatcher became prime minister. The rise in crime has occurred over roughly the same period, and has increased by roughly the same proportion, as the growth in the rates of divorce and illegitimacy discussed earlier.

In the view of Dennis and Erdos, these two trends are causally related. We know that most crime is committed by young males, and it seems plausible to suppose that many criminals have been inadequately socialized into norms and values which emphasize honesty, respect for others, and deference to the law. Dennis and Erdos provide evidence that children raised without fathers, or with uncommitted fathers, are more likely to be inadequately socialized than those raised by two committed parents, and they also show that such children are more likely to get into trouble with the police. They deduce from this that the decline in the traditional family is the major explanation for the rise in crime.

The problem with this argument, however, is that crime rates in Britain began to rise significantly in the late 1950s, slightly earlier than the rise in divorce rates, illegitimacy and unstable cohabitation. If changes in the family really were the crucial causal factor in changes in the crime rate, then we should expect a time lag of ten to fifteen years between them. The fact that these two trends developed in tandem suggests that there may be some third factor which explains them both.

One possible third factor is the emergence of the postwar welfare state. Universal state welfare was established in Britain from the mid-1940s, and both the crime rate and the decline in the conventional two-parent family began to rise a decade or so later. Furthermore, the welfare state was extended from the mid-1960s, and crime rates as well as divorce and illegitimacy rates then began to soar ten years after that. Much the same pattern can be seen in the United States following the introduction of the 'Great Society' reforms of the 1960s.[27]

This is not to suggest that state welfare directly causes crime and family breakdown, but it is possible that it has enabled these changes to occur. Single parenthood, for example, was not a viable option for most women before various welfare reforms from the 1960s onwards provided financial support for it. Similarly, there are financial incentives in the welfare system of the 1990s for the parents of a child to remain unmarried in order to take advantage of the various benefits available to lone mothers.[28] The stigma which surrounded illegitimacy thirty years ago has today been displaced by a range of welfare rights which have underpinned and normalized lifestyles which were previously deemed unacceptable.

The link between welfare and criminality is less readily established. The link, if there is one, is likely to involve various cultural changes associated with the extension of state welfare, and in particular the erosion of a traditional ethic of personal responsibility. As we shall see in Chapter 5, there are signs in both Britain and the United States that the old Protestant work ethic has been eroded, and that a new spirit of hedonism and narcissism, with an emphasis on immediate gratification, has grown up to fill the gap. Universal state welfare may well have contributed to this, for over the last fifty years welfare provision has broken the automatic link between personal effort (work and saving) and personal reward (income and consumption). In its place, it has established a right to income irrespective of personal behaviour or effort. In this way, modern welfare systems may unintentionally have contributed to the erosion of personal responsibility which is revealed in the increase in socially irresponsible behaviour since the late 1950s.[29]

Of course, criminality and the erosion of social responsibility are complex developments with multiple causes, and the welfare state is only one factor in these changes. What is clear, however, is that capitalism and the inequalities and acquisitiveness associated with it cannot of itself be held to blame. The Victorian period witnessed the high-point of liberal capitalism in England, yet crime rates actually fell during the second half of the nineteenth century. The interwar years witnessed the worst and most prolonged recession of the modern era, yet crime rates stayed very low throughout the 1920s and 1930s. It was only when capitalism was 'tamed' by large-scale state intervention after the war that crime began to rise significantly. Whatever the causes of this rise, it clearly makes no sense to attribute responsibility to the workings of a capitalist market economy.

This brings us to the third problem with Tönnies's critique of capitalism. The critique rests on the assumption that capitalism generates a culture of possessive individualism in which concern for others is subordinated to calculations of self-interest. However, a capitalist society can be either individualistic or communalistic in its culture, and there is nothing in the character of capitalism itself which necessarily generates one rather than the other.

There is a 'pervasive, powerful and persistent' belief that capitalism and individualism are inherently related, even though they originated separately and at different times.[30] Modern individualism originated in the Christian confessional of the thirteenth century where the individual was held morally responsible for his or her sins. It then developed through Renaissance art, with its emphasis on the literal representation of unique individuals, and through courtly rituals of behaviour. Reinforced by the legacy of Roman law, with its emphasis on individual rights and obligations, it eventually came to fruition in the writings of English philosophers such as Hobbes and Locke who emphasized individual rights as a radical challenge to the existing social order.

Individualistic ideas and practices were therefore already in place at the time when industrial capitalism began to take off in Britain in the eighteenth century. Although the development of capitalism further shaped the culture of individualism, Abercrombie and his co-authors insist that the two coincided only contingently at this one point in history. They also point out that, elsewhere in the world, even this fleeting link between individualism and early capitalism was absent. In Japan, for example, capitalism developed out of a strongly collectivistic Confucian culture and there is still a strongly collectivistic and nationalistic culture which infuses Japanese capitalism to this day.

Even in nineteenth-century Britain, however, everyday life was heavily permeated by communalistic values and behaviour. The Victorian middle classes had a strong commitment to charity and philanthropy which was underpinned by values emphasizing the 'social duty' owed to those less fortunate. The Victorian working classes likewise developed strong forms of communal activity expressed through the friendly societies and other organizations for mutual aid. It was only when government began to assume responsibility for 'improving the condition of the working classes' that the charitable work of the middle classes and the churches went into decline and the working-class culture of voluntarism and cooperation began to wither.[31]

We do not, therefore, need to look as far as Japan to find evidence of a communal culture coexisting with a capitalist economy. It happened in Britain at the high-point of liberal capitalism in the nineteenth century, but it occurred not at the level of the state, but through various 'intermediate institutions' such as churches and chapels, neighbourhoods and workplaces – the 'little platoons' of everyday life.[32] To the extent that this culture has disappeared, it is because the little platoons have been stripped of their function and their purpose by government action. The capitalist market system of nineteenth-century England gave rise to effective communalism, and the extension of modern 'citizenship rights' embodied in the twentieth-century welfare state destroyed it.[33]

Self-esteem and self-actualization

The final set of needs which we identified as necessary conditions for human happiness relate to a sense of self-worth and the ability to realize our particular capacities and potential in the things that we do. We have already seen that Marx believed that both were impossible under capitalist conditions, for workers cannot develop any sense of self-worth when their labour is routinely treated as a disposable commodity to be traded by others, and the scope for self-actualization is likewise curtailed when most workers are little more than 'flesh and blood appendages' to the machines they are obliged to operate.

One obvious response to this apparently powerful critique of capitalism is that the organization of work has changed dramatically since Marx's time due to the development of new technologies. There are two points here.

The first is that much of the dull, repetitive machine-minding characteristic of nineteenth-century industry has now disappeared, at least in the advanced capitalist countries, such that even manual labour now allows for more control and discretion by employees than was ever the case in the past. In his celebrated study of alienated labour, Robert Blauner[34] found that feelings of power-lessness, isolation and self-estrangement were much more associ-ated with machine and assembly line production than with more modern automated industries where workers are expected to exercise their own judgement and to assume considerable responsi-bility in their tasks. Moreover, since Blauner wrote his study, new 'post-Fordist' systems of production have encouraged greater flexibility in the use of labour within the factory, and this has increased the scope for workers to display autonomy and initia-tive.[35]

The second point is that factory work is itself in decline in all advanced capitalist countries. During the twentieth century, indus-trial employment has increasingly been displaced by the growth of the service sector, and manual labour has been replaced by non-manual occupations. In Britain in the early years following the First World War, some two-thirds of the workforce was employed in manufacturing. By 1993 the proportion had fallen to one-fifth.[36] Taken together with the decline in all forms of manual labour (down to 40 per cent of the workforce in Britain by 1993), these changes indicate that the factory proletariat which figures so centrally in Marx's writings is today only a small fraction of the total workforce in the mature capitalist economies.

Of course, many service sector jobs may provide no more opportunity for employees to exercise autonomy than the old factory jobs which they replaced – the monotony of life as a sales assistant in Woolworths or a hamburger chef in McDonald's can be almost as bad as the grinding tedium of the semi-skilled machine operative working in an old textile mill. There has been a major shift in employment towards managerial, administrative, professional and specialist technological occupations requiring relatively high levels of education and training and offering considerable scope for individuals to control their own work process and to exercise their talents in a relatively autonomous and challenging environment. But what of those individuals who still fill relatively menial and apparently unsatisfying positions in the occupational system? Does their experience of work prevent them from developing positive self-esteem and shut them off from the means for self-actualization?

A genuine sense of self-worth depends upon approval from others for the things that we do.[37] To be a source of genuine satisfaction, a high regard for self has to be earned; it is not a 'right' which can simply be asserted or which can be given to people irrespective of their own actions. This leads Murray to distinguish the 'self-esteem' which individuals may feel irrespective of how they behave, from the 'self-respect' which is the product of individuals accepting responsibility for their own actions and securing the approval of others who consider their behaviour worthy of high regard. In order to get self-respect you have to *do* something to earn it.

According to Murray, self-respect is perfectly possible for those in relatively menial jobs, just as much as for those in high-powered ones, for it depends upon behaviour rather than skill, education or income. Murray's argument is supported by ethnographic evidence from research on life in traditional proletarian communities in Britain[38] which has documented the strong sense of pride among men in their role as 'breadwinner', and among women in their role as 'housewife' and mother. Male self-respect in these communities was gained and maintained by prevailing over adversity, pulling your weight, being self-reliant, providing for your children, and not letting your workmates down. It had little or nothing to do with the content of the task performed at work which was often menial and arguably degrading. Similarly for women, self-respect was achieved by maintaining a clean home, turning out well-mannered children in neat attire, making ends meet so that there was always a meal on the table, and so on. These families were seen by their neighbours, and therefore saw themselves, as *respectable* working class, and they contrasted themselves with the 'rough' parts of town where the men failed to hold down a job, where the children were dirty and uncared for, and where family life often degenerated into a cycle of violence, dependency and alcohol abuse in the face of hardship and adversity.

It is clear from this that the existence of a class hierarchy does not in itself destroy the possibility for self-respect for those at the bottom.[39] Ultimately, it is not what people do for a living, but the way they live their lives, which matters for self-respect, which means that it is possible for any individual, no matter what his or her place in the occupational system, to live a life deemed worthy of respect by others (e.g. by being a good parent or a good neighbour).

Having recognized this, however, we have also to accept that in capitalist societies, occupational status is a key element in people's social identities and is a widely recognized sign of individual success and 'social honour'. It is possible to achieve self-respect by being a

good parent or a good neighbour, but it is success in the occupational system which provides the clearest sign of one's individual
worth. The question which this then raises is whether it is possible
for individuals born in lower social strata to improve themselves
through their own efforts and thereby to achieve the occupational
signs of success and self-respect.

Capitalism is in principle a system which allocates rewards
through open competition, but in the past those at the bottom were
often disadvantaged in this competition as compared with those at
the top. Before the Second World War, it was unusual for
working-class children in Britain to remain at school past the age of
14, still less to go to college or university, and although bright and
motivated individuals could and did 'work their way up' after
leaving school, relatively few could realistically aspire to a responsible or prestigious position. The contest was skewed, the dice were
loaded.

Many sociologists believe that little has changed, for children
from lower-class backgrounds are still less likely than those from
middle-class backgrounds to end up in middle-class occupations,
and the shortfall is generally taken as evidence of the continued
operation of class barriers against lower-class achievement.

There are remarkably high rates of social mobility in all the
advanced capitalist countries, but in every case the children of the
middle class tend to do better than those from the working class. In
Britain, a major study by John Goldthorpe[40] divided the population
into seven classes and found that movement up and down this class
structure was much more common than had generally been
thought. Upward movement by those born to working-class parents
was extensive, for only a quarter of men in class I had been born
there while 29 per cent had come from classes VI and VII. Similarly,
although 57 per cent of sons of working-class fathers had stayed in
the working class, 27 per cent of them had ended up in intermediate
positions and 16 per cent of them had risen into the 'service class'
(classes I and II). Goldthorpe also found that middle-class children
were not guaranteed success simply by virtue of their background.
While 59 per cent of sons of 'service class' fathers had retained their
class position, 26 per cent of them had fallen to 'intermediate'
positions and 15 per cent of them had fallen into the manual
working class. Given these findings, it is difficult to avoid the
conclusion that Britain looks a fairly open society.

Goldthorpe, however, remained sceptical, for he emphasized the apparent inequalities which still existed in the relative chances of success enjoyed by children from different backgrounds. Thus, he showed that the working-class child is a quarter or a third as likely to end up in the 'service class' as compared with the child who is born there, and he also demonstrated that this 'disparity ratio' of three or four to one was little different from that found in earlier generations. Arguing that in a genuinely open society there should be no statistical association between people's class of origin and their class of destination (a disparity ratio of one to one), he concluded that Britain remains a society in which the class system itself hinders the advancement of able and talented working-class people.

This conclusion only follows, however, if we accept that there exist no differences of aptitude between the members of different social classes in each generation. Goldthorpe's argument rests on the assumption that talent and effort are equally distributed between the classes, but in a meritocratic society, where recruitment is genuinely open and based solely on achievement, this is unlikely to be the case. This is because the most able people who end up in the top jobs in such a society will in turn tend to have relatively 'bright' children, while people of relatively lower ability who will be recruited to positions lower down the occupational hierarchy will in turn tend to produce children who are themselves on average less able. This being the case, a 'disparity ratio' of three or four to one, such as that found by Goldthorpe, would not be remarkable at all.

Elsewhere[41] I have shown that the pattern of intergenerational social mobility reported for Britain by Goldthorpe is almost exactly what one would predict under conditions of perfect meritocracy once differences of ability between parents in each class are allowed for. The implications of this are profound. The long-standing sociological belief that competition for middle-class positions is heavily weighted against working-class children must clearly be questioned, for it seems that individual ability and hard work may be what matter after all. If this is the case, then there are no grounds for arguing that contemporary capitalism prevents those who are good enough from achieving roles and positions which offer the prospect of justifiable self-esteem and self-respect, irrespective of the class into which they are born.

Where the occupational system under capitalism does seem to

militate against human happiness, however, is in its capacity to enable individuals to realize and develop their full potentials as human beings.

Murray argues that self-realization through work is a function of the complexity of the task undertaken relative to the skills and aptitudes of the person performing it. Too little stimulus creates boredom, but too much generates stress. For self-actualization to be maximized, it is therefore necessary to match up as far as possible the complexity of tasks with the ability of the individuals who perform them. There is no enjoyment to be gained from being asked to take on duties which are beyond one's ability to perform, just as there is little or no satisfaction to be had from performing tasks which one finds easy.

While we can readily accept the logic of this analysis, the problem clearly lies in the existence of jobs which are so routine or mundane that it is difficult to imagine them providing a stimulating challenge even to those of low intellectual ability. The scope for introducing meaningful creativity into such tasks is clearly very limited, and under capitalism there is anyway little incentive to organize the labour process to make it more creative.

Robert Lane has analysed this problem in some detail. He recognizes that the capitalist market system has proved adept at meeting people's needs as consumers, but he argues that it is work rather than consumption that offers the greater prospect for human fulfilment. It is here that capitalism has a problem, for it necessarily prioritizes the needs of consumers over those of workers, for 'consumers . . . are sovereign and those who work are their subjects'.[42]

Work enrichment under capitalism does occur, of course, and we have already seen that many of the most menial and degrading jobs have disappeared in the advanced capitalist countries as a result of new technologies. However, Lane points out that the reverse also occurs as jobs become 'deskilled' by the application of new technology to tasks which previously required craft, creativity and concentration. Moreover, job enrichment, when it does occur, can never be more than an incidental by-product of the introduction of new technologies and work practices aimed at raising efficiency and lowering unit costs. Whenever job satisfaction and efficient working practices come into conflict, it is the former which is necessarily sacrificed to the latter. As Lane explains

> Markets are excellent devices for the efficient production of goods
> and services; they are not designed for and have no special
> mechanism to promote human development. They neither necess-
> arily reward agents (firms) that do promote that kind of develop-
> ment, nor individuals who develop themselves.[43]

There can be little argument with Lane's view that self-
actualization through paid employment is systematically undervalued in capitalist societies, and that human happiness suffers as a
result. The only possible defence that can be offered for capitalism
against this critique is that people can and increasingly do seek
self-actualization outside paid employment, and that the development of modern capitalism makes this increasingly possible by
reducing the amount of time taken up by paid work and by
expanding the range of alternative activities which people can
choose to undertake.

The success of capitalism as a growth machine has had two
important consequences in this regard. First, it has reduced the
number of hours which people spend in paid work, not simply by
gradually reducing the length of the working week and extending
holiday entitlements, but also by delaying the initial entry of many
young people into the labour market (one-third of British 18-year-
olds now go on to higher education, for example) and by supporting
early retirement through choice, sickness or other factors. Second,
it has given individuals access to powerful means of production
which were earlier concentrated only in formal places of employment such as factories and offices. The widespread ownership of
washing machines, freezers, vacuum cleaners, lawnmowers, food
blenders, power drills, home computers, sewing machines and
other consumer durables has given the average household today a
greater command over horsepower than was available to the
average factory operative a hundred years ago.[44]

These sorts of goods are not simply consumed passively in the
home, but are used actively by households to produce further goods
and services for themselves.[45] Even an apparently passive tool like a
video recorder is used by households to provide their own 'cinema
service' which plays the film they want to see under circumstances
which they control. The spread of all this domestic technology is
said by Gershuny to be creating a new 'self-service' economy in
which productive and creative work can occur as much outside
formal employment as within it.

Not everybody, of course, can afford to participate in rewarding forms of domestic production, although most of the technology required is relatively cheap and ownership of most consumer durables extends widely across all income groups and social classes. We have also to remember that some of the work which people carry out for themselves at home can be just as tedious and unrewarding as that carried out in factories and offices, although much of it is voluntarily undertaken and is experienced by men and women alike as creative and fulfilling. In his path-breaking study of domestic self-provisioning in a working-class area in southern England, Ray Pahl concluded that, while some of it is undertaken reluctantly by people with insufficient funds to purchase the services they require from outside, much of it is done because it 'provides aesthetic satisfactions, pride in workmanship and a sense of domestic solidarity'.[46]

All of this suggests that Lane's focus on paid employment as the key source of self-actualization may have been misdirected. While it is true that workers often fail to develop their full capacities in their jobs, it does not follow from this that they are thereby prevented from achieving effective self-realization in other areas of their lives which may actually be more important to them. As Hugh Stretton has suggested, modern capitalism may not have overcome the problem of self-actualization within paid labour, but it has opened up the possibility of achieving the same result by another route: 'The revolutionized domestic sector does away with precisely the aspects of alienation and exploitation that Marx denounced'.[47]

Assuming that the capitalist growth machine keeps on producing growth, we may predict that the centrality of paid work in many people's lives will continue to recede and that the possibilities for pursuing self-actualization through other forms of work will correspondingly continue to expand. If this happens, then it is conceivable that capitalism could overcome the last and most intractable of the requirements necessary to enable individuals to achieve happy and fulfilling lives. The long-standing promise of security, fraternity, dignity, individual fulfilment and relief from the pain of material want which was once held out as a dream by nineteenth-century socialists may well be within the reach of twenty-first-century capitalism.

5

The Future of Capitalism

It is often suggested that capitalism is an unplanned system. It would, however, be more accurate to say that it is a system involving devolved planning, for capitalist firms employ a whole battery of accountants, financial advisers, market analysts, sales directors, strategic planners, systems analysts and human resources directors to help them plan every aspect of their operations. Their problem, however, is that the market environment in which they plan is inherently unpredictable. Because firms must compete for customers whose future purchasing decisions are unknown, they can never be sure whether they are producing the right volume of the right product at the right time. Patterns of consumer demand can and do shift as new products come on to the market, as fashions change, and as people's incomes go up or down, and invention of new technologies can rapidly render existing production lines obsolete. As we saw in Chapter 1, this unrelenting competition for market shares is what makes capitalism so dynamic, for it keeps all firms on their toes, but it also makes it a hazardous system for company shareholders and employees.

It was this chronic instability of the market which led Karl Marx to his prediction that capitalism would eventually destroy itself. Marx identified a whole series of 'crisis tendencies' within market capitalism, but his key thesis was that competition would inexorably lead to ever increasing rates of technological innovation which would drive smaller firms out of business and which would reduce the rate of profit in the economy as a whole as labour was progressively replaced by machines. As production became concentrated in a small number of huge corporations, so the mass of the population would become fused into a huge proletariat with no stake in the system. At some point in the future, this proletariat would simply reach out and remove the means of production from the hands of the tiny capitalist class which remained. History would come to an end as the whole population for the first time owned and controlled the productive assets on which all their lives depended.

The end of history?

Marx's great prophecy has not, of course, come to pass, nor is it likely to. His prediction that capital would become concentrated through a series of competitive take-overs and buy-outs has happened to some extent, for we now live in a world of huge corporations organized across whole continents, but it is not true that new firms cannot arise to challenge these monsters, nor is it the case that ownership of the corporations is limited to a small number of people.

Many of the most successful companies today are new firms which have taken on the established giants. Bill Gates, who founded Microsoft in the 1970s is now the richest individual in the United States, and nearly three-quarters of the 500 richest individuals in Britain amassed their fortunes by their own efforts, many of them through manufacturing.[1] Furthermore, ownership of capital is today diffused as never before, for millions of people save or invest with insurance companies, pension funds and other financial institutions which invest their monthly payments in shareholdings and other forms of capital and which redeem their policies through profits gained from these investments. Far from having 'nothing to lose but their chains', the mass of the population in the advanced capitalist countries today has a huge stake in the continued profitability of capitalist enterprises.

There are no grounds today for predicting an apocalyptic crash in which capitalism finally disappears, nor can we any more envisage a situation in which the 'popular masses' rise up to seize control of the means of production. Nevertheless, capitalist economies do still lurch from boom to slump and back again, much as Marx described a hundred years ago. In the absence of any overall mechanism for planning production, it is only through periodic recessions that a market system can shut down activities which have become obsolete or uncompetitive and redirect labour and capital into new ones.

Governments have over the years tried to do something about this, but short of taking the whole system into state ownership (a strategy which failed spectacularly in eastern Europe), there is little they can do other than to put in place welfare systems designed to pick up the pieces.

The Keynesian fix of the postwar years, in which governments tried to flatten out the booms and soften the slumps by deflating or inflating consumer demand, collapsed ignominiously in the 1970s in an unprecedented combination of soaring inflation and escalating unemployment. Attempts at planning trade, managing exchange rates or manipulating interest rates have likewise run up against powerful market forces which have sooner or later left such strategies in tatters. Since the 1970s, most governments have come to realize that their economies are plugged into a global system over which they can exercise little effective influence or control, although this has still not stopped them trying.[2]

Meanwhile, new threats have emerged to the established capitalist economies. Rapid economic growth in the countries of the Far East poses a major problem for the United States and the European Union, for while these countries represent new markets into which to sell western products, they also dramatically undercut American and European labour costs and they entice western capital to invest there rather than at home. Competition from Japan since the 1960s has knocked out whole areas of British industry including motor cycles, televisions and even cars, and throughout western Europe and North America manufacturing employment has gone into precipitate decline. Such problems are only likely to be multiplied by the emergence of China and the smaller nations of Asia as major centres of world manufacturing.

The collapse of socialism in eastern Europe poses similar problems closer to home. This has created not only political instability in several of the former Soviet republics and in areas such as the former Yugoslavia, but also a huge new region of low-wage market economies with which the established countries will now have to compete. Changes in eastern Europe also threaten to trigger a wave of migration westwards as people seek to share in the relative prosperity of countries such as Germany which is already struggling to meet the costs of unification and whose problems have destabilized other European Union economies. All this instability has helped fuel a resurgence of racism throughout Europe as government budgets come under increasing pressure and the competition for jobs intensifies. Capitalism is not about to collapse, but in the West it is under considerable strain.

These threats and tensions are the product of capitalism's success in establishing itself on a global scale. Both the competition from Asia and the problems posed by the collapse of socialism in eastern Europe represent threats to the postwar prosperity and stability of the core western capitalist nations, but they are the product of capitalism's success in finally establishing itself as a world system unchallenged by any viable alternative. The difficulties which capitalism faces today are not the harbingers of its impending collapse, as in Marx's predictions, but are the problems associated with its ultimate triumph.

In 1989, just a few months before the breach of the Berlin Wall, Francis Fukuyama, an American State Department policy planner, published an essay entitled 'The End of History?' which seemed to many to capture the essence of a major change which was beginning to make itself felt throughout the world. Boldly snatching Marx's Hegelian clothing, Fukuyama announced that we were now present at the end of history:

> What we may be witnessing is not just the end of the Cold War, or the passing of a particular period of postwar history, but the end of history as such: that is, the end point of mankind's ideological evolution and the universalization of Western liberal democracy as the final form of human government.[3]

He argued that, for much of the twentieth century, economic and political liberalism had been under threat from alternative totali-tarian systems of thought represented by fascism and socialism. The faith in liberalism, which had characterized western thought before the First World War, had been eroded through much of this period as intellectuals forecast either the replacement of liberal capitalism by world socialism, or a global 'convergence' in which the logic of industrialism would lead socialist and capitalist countries alike into some sort of middle ground involving extensive state control and regulation of economic and social life. Only at the end of the twentieth century has western liberalism regained its self-confidence, for by 1989 it was clear that all viable alternative systems had been exhausted.

The power of the fascist ideal was killed off in 1945 by the occupation of Berlin and the atom bombs dropped on Japan, while the power of the communist ideal has more recently been killed off by the abandonment of Marxism as a guide to policy in China and by the sudden collapse of the Soviet Union. Fukuyama recognized that the liberal ideal was still some way from fulfilment in many parts of the world (China, for example, continues to be governed by an extremely illiberal regime), but his thesis required only that there be an end to alternative ideologies with a realistic claim to represent a different and 'higher' form of social organization. By 1989, he believed that the world had reached this point. We have reached the end of history because it is clear that there is now nothing left to challenge or replace the liberal idea.

The only possible future challenges which Fukuyama could detect were from religious fundamentalism and from a resurgence of nationalism. Neither, however, poses a fundamental threat to western liberalism, for the theocratic regimes of the Islamic world have little widespread appeal outside the Muslim countries, while new nationalist movements are limited in their aims to liberation from control by other racial or ethnic groups and do not generally seek to usher in new forms of political and economic organization. Fukuyama recognized that conflicts may continue to occur, particularly between those states which remain 'locked into history' and those which have reached the end of it (the Gulf War is a good example), but he predicted an end to the grand ideologies which have thrown the world into conflict in the past. With the end of history, people would become much more preoccupied with economics than with politics, with resolving technical problems rather than with realizing heroic dreams. The end of history, he warned, offered the prospect of 'centuries of boredom'.[4]

Any attempt at evaluating Fukuyama's thesis should first bear in mind the necessary caution which we should bring to any bold vision proclaiming how the future is likely to unfold. The same philosophical difficulties which beset Marx's historicism apply equally to Fukuyama's, for we cannot know the future and it is dangerous simply to extrapolate forward from current trends which can rapidly reverse themselves taking us all by surprise. As Max Weber understood, and as Fukuyama seems to have forgotten, social life is always characterized by the clash between ultimate values, 'warring gods' which charge the human imagination and which give ultimate meaning to human actions.[5] It would therefore be surprising if politics were to degenerate in the future into a series of technical fixes, or if there were to emerge no new ideologies to confront the unheroic formal rationality of liberal market systems. Indeed, we saw in Chapter 3 that there are already signs that the vacuum left by the collapse of the socialist ideal may come to be filled by the populist appeal of deep green ideologies, for the apparent threat of environmental annihilation can be used to justify grand schemes of social and economic reconstruction in which the flickering flame of liberalism would soon be extinguished.

We should, therefore, be sceptical about the claim that we have reached the end of history. We should also be wary of assuming that Fukuyama's thesis demonstrates the triumph of liberal capitalism as opposed to the more bureaucratic or corporatist forms which characterize many capitalist countries outside the United States. Fukuyama writes of the triumph of the western liberal ideal, in economics and in politics, but many of the most successful capitalist economies are not organized on liberal principles and there is anyway no necessary relationship between a market economy and a liberal democratic form of polity.[6] Furthermore, as we shall see later, it is far from certain that the liberal ideal has been revitalized by a new spirit of self-confidence even within the core capitalist nations.

There is a worrying ethnocentrism in Fukuyama's implicit assumption that the victory of capitalism represents a victory for the western, and in particular the American, form of capitalism. Ideologues of the free market have found in Fukuyama's essay a justification for arguing that the nineteenth-century liberal ideal is about to make a comeback on a global scale. There is, however, precious little evidence to support this, for the triumph of capitalism does not necessarily represent a triumph for the free market. Fukuyama's work is fundamentally flawed by its failure to recognize that there is more than one kind of capitalism which has survived the ideological upheavals of the twentieth century.

Capitalism versus capitalism

With the demise of the threat of socialism, American-style capitalism is now challenged by an alternative model of capitalism which the United States itself helped to nurture in the aftermath of the Second World War. Albert has identified this alternative form of capitalism as the 'Rhine model', for it is associated mainly with countries such as Germany, Switzerland and the Netherlands, although elements of this model are also found in Scandinavia and, most crucially, Japan. He contrasts it with what he calls the 'neo-American' model whose homeland is the United States but which is also found to some extent in other Anglo-Saxon countries including Britain.[7]

We have already seen signs of the divergence between these two different capitalist systems in Chapter 4, where the contrast was drawn between the emphasis on individual success, competition and short-term financial gain in the United States, and the importance of collective success, cooperation and longer-term concerns in countries such as Germany and Japan. This is not the only difference between them, however. Albert shows, for example, that there is a greater emphasis on training in the Rhine model, and that firms in the neo-American model tend to rely heavily on capital raised in the stock markets while those in the Rhine model rely much more on loans from banks with which they enjoy a close and long-term relationship. Income distribution also tends to be more unequal, and state welfare tends to be much less developed in the neo-American model, although on this latter indicator Japan comes closer to the United States and Britain comes closer to Germany.

Albert is in no doubt which of these models is proving the more successful: 'In the last decade or so, it is this Rhine model . . . that has shown itself to be the more efficient of the two, as well as the more equitable'.[8] He points out that US capitalism has enormous competitive advantages including a legacy of huge capital investment from the past, vast reserves of raw materials and energy, the attraction of many of the best brains in the world, a cultural hegemony based upon English as the world language of business and popular culture, and a world reserve currency which has allowed the US government to print up to $500 billion without ever having to redeem the bills which continue to circulate beyond its borders. Yet despite all this, America is performing badly on a wide range of indicators.

As in Britain, so in the United States, manufacturing industry is in decline and many of the new jobs which have been created are in low-paid service employment. American manufacturing output has now been overtaken by Japan. By the end of 1990, the United States had become the world's biggest debtor with a government budget deficit of over $3 trillion (equivalent to three years of government revenue from all sources). Socially, the American cities are blighted by homelessness, drug abuse and crime, while infant mortality rates are twice as high in America as in Japan. And culturally, a long-standing crisis in the American schooling system has resulted in American children scoring lowest of all industrial countries in their knowledge of science, in more than half of all American adults being unable to place Britain, France or Japan on a world map, and in an adult illiteracy rate higher than it is in Poland. All of this, according to Albert, indicates 'an increasingly fragmented and uncaring society of dysfunctional families and spreading poverty'.[9]

Albert sees the root cause of the problem in the American culture of individualism. This, he believes, was counter-balanced for a long time by a strong social consensus based on religious morality and a widespread commitment to the sanctity of the Constitution, but these ethical foundations have now been eroded, and all that is left is naked self-interest and the pursuit of the fast buck. As we saw in Chapter 4, capitalism cannot sustain a healthy society of happy individuals unless it is underpinned by some sort of shared moral framework. In Albert's view, this is no longer the case in the neo-American model of capitalism where honour and trust have disappeared and the system has degenerated into selfishness and corruption. In the United States, the captains of industry pay themselves 110 times as much as the average pay of their employees. This compares with a multiplier of just 23 in Germany and 17 in Japan.

Americans have stopped saving. Savings in the United States fell from 19 per cent of GDP in 1980 to 13 per cent ten years later. In Germany, by contrast, savings rose from 22 per cent to 26 per cent over the same period, and in Japan they increased from 31 per cent to 35 per cent. Instead of saving, the Americans, like the British, have become a nation of credit card consumers and short-term speculators. The new American heroes are men like Donald Trump and Ivan Boesky who make millions of dollars dealing in junk bonds which are used to buy up undervalued companies and strip them of their assets. The old middle-class ethic of hard work and long-term investment has simply disappeared.

Unlike the Rhine model countries, where the banks lend long-term to companies to enable them to invest in new products which may not show an immediate profit, the neo-American model relies on funding from the stock market which places a premium on short-run rates of return. The result is that companies have to maintain a flow of dividends to shareholders for fear of being taken over by corporate raiders, and long-term planning therefore goes by the board. The huge financial institutions which together own the controlling interest in most major British and American companies can switch their investments from low- to high-yielding shares with devastating results for the companies they abandon, and this has created a climate of volatility and uncertainty which militates against good business practice. 'The tyranny of finance', concludes Albert, 'is threatening the spirit of free enterprise'.[10]

In the Rhine model of capitalism, individual self-interest is leavened by a strong culture of collective responsibility and consensus. Albert maintains that this system is still based on free trade, but that the operation of the law and the activities of government ensure greater stability and economic cooperation. In Germany, for example, the hostile take-over bid is virtually unknown, and one-third of companies issue only 'registered shares' which cannot be sold or transferred without the company's permission. It is the Bundesbank's commitment to maintaining a strong currency, rather than the perpetual threat of take-overs, which keeps German industry efficient, and manufacturing in Germany still accounts for 30 per cent of GDP as compared with less than 20 per cent in the United States.

There is a strong emphasis on training in the Rhine model. The system of lifetime employment in large Japanese companies means that firms are willing to invest in training their workers without having to worry about losing them to a rival company, and in Germany, about half of all school leavers enter apprenticeships as compared with just 14 per cent in Britain. In Japan, companies also provide many aspects of welfare for their employees, while the German *Sozialmarktwirtschaft* is underpinned by a government commitment to providing a strong social security system, welfare services financed mainly through direct taxation, good urban transport and a strong system of state education. While the market is left to determine prices and wages, the German government imposes duties on employers regarding employee participation and working conditions, and it seeks to maintain a 'level

playing field' by regulating monopolies, offering tax breaks to
smaller companies, and providing aid for the poorer regions.[11]

Although holiday entitlements and working hours in Japan are
still less generous than in the West, Germany enjoys the shortest
working hours and the highest wages of all the leading capitalist
countries. As in Japan, German trade unions cooperate with employers (and with consumer organizations) in joint management
teams which help foster a strong sense of corporate belonging and
company loyalty. Social inequalities are much smaller than in the
neo-American model, and Germany has been much more successful than the United States in combating poverty and social depri-
vation.

Albert leaves us in no doubt that the Rhine model is outper-
forming the neo-American one. Despite this, however, he recognizes that it is the neo-American model which is in the ascendant,
for there are signs in Germany, Japan and elsewhere that company
structures are changing, that the welfare consensus is under strain,
and that the traditional role of the banks in financing investment is
being challenged by increasing reliance on stock market funding.
One reason for these changes lies in the globalization of the financial markets following the introduction of new communications
technologies and the invention of new financial instruments such as
the futures markets in currencies. For Albert, the globalization of
finance represents the means by which Wall Street and the City of
London have been able to infiltrate and undermine the Rhine
model.

There are, however, at least two other reasons why the Rhine
model is under threat, and these reflect inherent weaknesses within
the model itself. One is economic, the other cultural.

The economic factor is simply that Rhine capitalism is a high-cost
system which is finding it hard to compete with the newly emerging
low-cost capitalist economies in Asia and elsewhere. In a world
where there is an increasing emphasis on free trade, it is proving increasingly difficult for efficient Rhine model countries such as Germany to pay for their high wages and expensive social provisions
purely out of efficiency gains, and the new capitalist countries in
Asia are winning increased market shares by undercutting them. In
a world where traditionally poor countries are looking to compete
in capitalist markets, the Rhine model of capitalism looks increasingly vulnerable unless it retreats behind ever higher tariff walls.

The second factor which helps explain why the apparently less efficient neo-American model may still end up triumphant has to do with its greater cultural tolerance of individual diversity and freedom. Albert himself hints at this when he recognizes that the Rhine model seems somewhat devoid of glamour and excitement. 'Rhine capitalism', he admits, 'suffers from an image problem: it looks out of date, it breeds neither dreams nor excitement, it is not fun'.[12] Albert puts this down to the cultural hegemony of Hollywood and the American media which have successfully pedalled a glitzy image of American capitalism across the world. He believes that the popular appeal of American-style liberal capitalism is based on nothing more than 'star quality', that it is a system with style but no substance. But the popular appeal of the neo-American model rests on more than just media images.

Albert himself recognizes that countries such as the United States and Britain have tended to be more open and more tolerant of individual diversity than countries such as Japan and Germany. He cites the example of immigration, where both Britain and the United States have historically been much more receptive to immigrants and have extended citizenship rights to newcomers much more readily than is the case in countries which have developed the Rhine model of capitalism. Immigrants to Britain and America have often been treated badly, but they have not been denied citizenship in the way that the German nationality laws have prevented Turkish *Gastarbeiter* from claiming basic civil rights even after years of settled residence. Nor do British and American municipalities have the legal right to enforce ethnic residence quotas such as those in German cities where new immigrants can be banned from living in neighbourhoods where there are already high levels of ethnic minority concentration. Even today, immigration restrictions in Britain and America seem relatively liberal when compared with Rhine countries such as Switzerland where it is virtually impossible for immigrants to settle.

Albert accepts that the Rhine model is less open and more rigid, and that it is therefore much more resistant to other cultures and much less inclined to adapt to them. Mixed-race marriages are much less common in Germany and Japan, for example, than they are in the United States and Britain. All this reflects the fact that Rhine capitalism has been built upon fundamentally conservative national cultures in which individual diversity is valued much less highly than collective conformity. This makes for efficient capitalism but it sits uneasily with a liberal culture.

The differences regarding immigration and nationality laws are just one of a number of indicators of this cultural divergence between the two systems. There is, for example, a strong libertarian resistance to the introduction of identity cards in Britain, yet these have never been a problem in most of continental Europe where all adults are obliged to register their address with the police whenever they move home. Peacetime conscription is a feature of virtually every capitalist country grouped under Albert's category of the Rhine model yet is conspicuously absent from those, including Britain, Australia and the United States, which correspond more closely to the neo-American variant. In Germany, the Benelux countries and Scandinavia all young males have to perform national service of some kind, and in Switzerland every adult male must register for military duty each year up until the age of 55 as well as joining a local rifle club to maintain his shooting skills. There is a cultural resistance to these sorts of requirements in the neo-American cultures where the value of individualism is more entrenched and where there is a traditional concern to maintain a clear separation between political authority and civil society.

It seems that the 'unorganized' quality of Anglo-Saxon capitalism which results in greater economic inefficiency nevertheless helps to avoid the tendency to social conformity and uniformity which characterizes many Rhine model countries. As Durkheim recognized, modern societies need to steer a course between the 'anomie' of normative deregulation and the 'fatalism' born of too strong a commitment to social rules and common objectives.[13] If the neo-American model veers towards the first of these pathologies, it can be argued that the Rhine model veers too far towards the second.

In Japan, for example, the company paternalism which creates the security of lifetime employment expresses and reinforces a level of social conformity which is astonishing viewed through western eyes. The conformity which is fostered in the schools, where the 'cramming system' emphasizes rote learning at the expense of self-expression, is later reinforced in the workplace. Japanese companies have their own anthems which they expect their employees to memorize, and they run sports and social clubs which they expect their employees to join. They have their own moral codes stressing 'enthusiasm for work and vigorous play, healthy extraverted camaraderie, serious-mindedness, patriotism, honesty, clean living and high thinking',[14] and these are promoted through company magazines and in weekend outings which employees are expected to attend. This is a culture which is well adapted to producing a hard-working, loyal and conformist workforce, but it is rather less successful at producing free-thinking individuals. Japan has succeeded in flooding the world with cheap and reliable Sony Walkmans, but it has been much less successful in generating Nobel Prize winners, and it struggles to compete with countries like the United States in creative fields such as the production of new computer software.

The legacy of the samurai bands of the Tokugawa period can still be found in the culture of modern Japanese corporations. This is a society where individualism is distrusted, where employees are expected to put the interests of the company above those of their own families, and where there was until recently no word in the language to express the idea of 'privacy' without simultaneously implying either 'selfishness' or 'loneliness'. As Ron Dore suggests, there is no space in a society like this for the development of the western liberal ideal in which morally responsible individuals make their own judgements about how best to behave and which ethical precepts they should follow: 'Man-imbedded-in-organization has no great need to make personal moral choices; the organization's norms set guidelines; the organization's sanctions keep him to the path of virtue'.[15]

In Europe, too, the Rhine model of capitalism seems to coexist with cultures in which individual autonomy is discouraged and individual diversity is distrusted. In Sweden, the government's commitment since the 1930s to providing economic security for all its citizens has been part of a broader project intended to build unity through conformity. Those who deviate from official norms of behaviour (e.g. by drinking more alcohol than is deemed good for them) have been closely monitored by state agencies with the power to impose 'treatment' upon them, even if they have broken no laws, and criminal behaviour is considered more as an aberrant 'illness' than as the product of individuals exercising free will and making their own moral choices. Until recently, policies in housing, education, employment and welfare all quite consciously sought to foster a uniform culture, expressed in the ideal of the *folkshelm*, in which everybody could feel a sense of belonging but in which nobody could be allowed to be too different. The same culture which gave us efficient Volvo factories turning out ultra-safe Volvo cars also produced an acceptance of collective interference in many areas of personal life which in Britain or America would seem intolerable.[16]

In another of the Rhine model countries, Switzerland, order is even more firmly maintained. As in Japan and Sweden, the government explicitly uses the schools to foster the norms and values which it sees as appropriate to its citizens, and these standards are then vigorously enforced, if necessary by law. In seven cantons it is illegal for unmarried couples to live together, and under Swiss law parents who are deemed negligent can lose control of their children without any recourse to the courts. Moreover, conformity in Switzerland is maintained not simply by the police and the immigration officials but by citizens themselves, for this is a self-policing society in which collective moral standards are enforced through high levels of informal surveillance. As an official of the Bern Youth Authority has suggested: 'There is no country in the world with more rules, more intolerance. Everybody in Bern is a village policeman and in Zurich it is even worse'.[17]

Rhine capitalism has, then, been so successful economically in large part because it has tapped into and reinforced national cultures which are relatively conformist. Planned and regulated capitalism can flourish in societies which produced Calvin or Hegel, but it is always going to look out of place in a culture which spawned John Stuart Mill and the Rolling Stones.

As we saw in Chapter 4, capitalism is not necessarily linked with individualism, but in countries like Britain and the United States individualistic values appear far more deeply entrenched than in Germany and Japan. This may well be a problem for today's big corporations which require a high degree of predictability and conformity, for the spirit of individualism is in many respects incompatible with the requirements of modern, corporate capitalism.[18] For individuals, however, the romantic appeal of these cultures is not difficult to understand, and the ability of neo-American capitalism to inspire popular enthusiasm cannot entirely be explained, as Albert would have us believe, by the myth-making industry of Hollywood.

Postindustrial capitalism and postmodern culture

There are signs, however, that the culture of individual responsibility and self-reliance in the Anglo-Saxon capitalist countries is under threat. One of the key observations made by Albert in his critique of neo-American capitalism is that the traditional values which used to underpin this system have been disintegrating. The emphasis on individual rights and liberties is still strong, but the corresponding emphasis on personal initiative and social responsibility seems to be collapsing. Everybody knows his or her rights, but few accept the obligations which go with them. Albert puts this change down to the decline of religion, but the causes probably lie much deeper than that.

One of the first sociologists to recognize this trend was Joseph Schumpeter. As early as 1943, he argued that bourgeois culture in the United States was in terminal decline as a result of two crucial developments. The first was that capitalist property had become depersonalized with the growth of huge corporations. This 'evaporation of the substance of property' has eroded independent entrepreneurship and has replaced it by a faceless form of managerialism which can no longer inspire moral commitment: 'Dematerialized, defunctionalized and absentee ownership does not impress and call forth moral allegiance as the vital form of property did. Eventually there will be nobody left who really cares to stand for it'.[19]

The second development was that the spirit of rational critique which capitalism had initially unleashed against the feudal order was now being turned upon itself. By fostering the growth of a knowledge society, capitalism has created a new, educated, class which has no direct responsibility for practical affairs but which has a vested interest in criticizing the existing order and in challenging the ethics on which it is based. For this class, nothing is sacrosanct, and nothing is beyond criticism. Religion is attacked as archaic, the bourgeois family is rejected as patriarchal, private property is dismissed as immoral, and ambition, competition, saving and personal effort are scorned as stultifying. Capitalism has thus created a class of opinion leaders who no longer believe in or endorse the traditional bourgeois values of hard work, individual effort, family responsibility and Christian charity. The influence of this class, not only on the masses but even on the bourgeoisie itself, is pernicious and profound, for even the capitalist class is losing faith in its own creed.

For Schumpeter, therefore, the development of huge corporations was eroding the legitimacy of capitalist property at exactly the same time as a new class was arising to challenge its moral authority. This analysis was remarkably prescient, for the expansion of higher education and the increase in middle-class service employment since the Second World War has enormously expanded the influence of this new class, and the impact of its increasingly critical stand against bourgeois values has been substantial.

The twentieth-century 'revolt against reason', triggered by the writings of Nietzsche and Sorel, led many social affairs intellectuals to abandon their faith in rationality and progress.[20] Cognitive relativism (the denial of any objective basis for distinguishing truth from falsity) swiftly spawned a belief in moral relativism, in which absolute judgements of right and wrong are attacked, and any attempt to assert the superiority of one set of moral standards over another is seen as suspect. The result is that the old moral consensus, shared in common by the middle classes and the 'respectable' working class alike, has been shattered. Attempts to resurrect it, as in Margaret Thatcher's call in the 1980s for a return to 'Victorian values', John Major's policy in the 1990s of 'back to basics', or Dan Quayle's attack on the 'lax moral standards' portrayed in American soap operas, meet today with a barrage of indignant criticism from social affairs intellectuals who deny that there are any moral certainties, and who assert the right of all individuals to pursue whichever lifestyle they prefer, irrespective of its viability or its long-term social consequences. Today, anything goes, and only censoriousness is censured.

In this way, the liberal tradition of toleration of diversity has degenerated into what Daniel Bell has diagnosed as a culture of self-gratification based on an irrational and unrestrained spirit of individualism.[21] The Puritan emphasis on work as a vocation has disappeared and the traditional sobriety of the middle and 'respectable' working classes finds little support in a dominant intellectual culture which emphasizes immediate gratification and the narcissistic pursuit of pleasure and personal desires. Mass consumption, fuelled by an explosion of credit, has displaced the old 'goodness morality', in which happiness and individual reward were linked to work and moral virtue, and has replaced it with a 'fun morality', in which any failure to achieve instant gratification becomes the cause for anxious self-examination and a visit to one's analyst. There is no longer any widely held set of moral values which can legitimate the bourgeois lifestyle, and the spirit of individualism which previously underpinned economic activity within capitalism now undermines it. Work is seen as an irrelevant and irksome hindrance to gratification, rather than as a means to its fulfilment, and concern with individual virtue is disregarded as archaic or smug.

So far have these developments gone that we have today normalized and legitimized behaviour which was once regarded as abnormal and illegitimate, while stigmatizing and discrediting behaviour which was once normal and respectable.[22] Virginity past the age of 15 has become an embarrassment, belief in God and commitment to a Christian lifestyle is seen as quaint, exclusive heterosexuality is seen as narrow, low-paid work is spurned as undignified, social security fraud is accepted as legitimate, marriage is regarded as outdated, and the traditional 'housewife' who stays at home to look after her children has become an object of pity. Values once associated with the 'underclass' are now endorsed as acceptable and unexceptional. The old bourgeois ethic has been turned on its head in a remarkably short period of time by the development of what sociologists have come to call 'postmodern' culture.[23]

In the postmodern era, we have no confidence in the correctness of our own moral judgements and we therefore shy away from judging others. Even government has become morally relativistic, decoupling welfare provision from any duty on the part of the recipients to behave in a certain way or to assume any responsibility for their own condition. The language of moral duty has fallen into disuse. Today, there are only different lifestyle choices, each equally valid, and ethics has become a matter of individual taste, for there are no longer any 'meta-narratives' against which to judge the competing claims of a plurality of world-views and ways of life. Everything has to be tolerated, nothing can be ruled out, nobody is wrong, and it is 'society' rather than individuals which is held to blame when the choice of unsustainable lifestyles produces personal unhappiness and misery. The legacy of liberalism has been betrayed by those who have plundered it as a licence for moral abdication.[24]

Both Schumpeter and Bell believed that they were witnessing the end of the bourgeois era. No less than any other socio-economic system, capitalism needs a shared moral framework within which to operate. It needs individuals to be motivated to act in certain ways, it needs symbols to legitimate the inequalities of condition which arise from market transactions, and it needs a core set of values which can bind people together through ties of mutual obligation and social responsibility. Nineteenth-century liberals such as John Stuart Mill believed that such a morality would be secure in a society of strong and free individuals, for he could not believe that educated and rational human beings would fail to understand how individual freedom depends upon respect for others and how the self-interest of each demands a recognition of social duty and obligation by all.[25] Today, Mill's faith stands exposed as utopian and his utilitarian ethics have been swept away in a torrent of relativism and anti-rationalism.

None of this is to deny that contemporary capitalism can still be defended and justified through an appeal to absolute moral values. Faced with mounting evidence of moral fragmentation in countries such as Britain and the United States, neo-conservative intellectuals have recently devoted considerable effort to demonstrating that the capitalist market system is consistent with Judaeo-Christian ethics, and that the profit motive does not imply a disregard for the needs of others.[26] The real significance of these publications, however, is that these writers now feel the need to make these arguments explicit, for this itself indicates how far the 'common-sense' wisdom has been eroded. In our postmodern culture, there is room for those who wish to reassert old moralities, just as much as for those who seek to explore new ones (or, indeed, those who see no need for any philosophy of ethics at all). Of course capitalism can be defended in intellectual-moral argument. What is significant, however, is that this argument should be happening at all, for no one position is any longer assumed to be privileged.

In the postmodern era, there are no clear answers which parents or teachers or politicians can give (assuming even that they wished to) to those who ask why they should sacrifice current earnings to train for a career, why they should tie themselves down for twenty years to raise the children they produce, why they should respect the property of others rather than take it for themselves, why they should accept the obligations of citizenship rather than simply asserting their rights to welfare support, why they should defer to authority or recognize established rules of behaviour rather than go their own way and do their own thing, or why they should seek to be self-reliant, to take pride in their achievements, to recognize their obligations and to fulfil their responsibilities.

Yet in the absence of clear, authoritative and unambiguous answers to these questions, the survival of the capitalist system in the liberal western countries is thrown into doubt. It would indeed be ironic if, at the 'end of history', when all alternative social visions have collapsed and when other parts of the world are busily engaged in developing and extending their own capitalist forms of enterprise, the core capitalist countries of the West were simply to degenerate through cultural exhaustion. The portents of such a decline are nevertheless present, and there seems little that government or anybody else can do to reverse them. Fukuyama, it seems, got it wrong, for rather than a new self-confidence in the liberal vision of modernity, we are witnessing today a loss of faith in the historic liberal values of social progress and individual enlightenment which enabled western capitalism to survive and then prevail over all alternative systems in the first place.

Notes

Chapter 1

1 See E. Hobsbawm, *The Age of Revolution* (London: Weidenfeld & Nicolson, 1962), p. 52.
2 This is noted by E. Hobsbawm, *The Age of Capital* (London: Weidenfeld & Nicolson, 1975), and by T. Bottomore, *Theories of Modern Capitalism* (London: George Allen & Unwin, 1985).
3 M. Mann, 'European Development: Approaching a Historical Explanation' in J. Baechler, J. Hall and M. Mann (eds), *Europe and the Rise of Capitalism* (Oxford: Basil Blackwell, 1988).
4 See M. Dobb, *Studies in the Development of Capitalism*, 2nd edn (London: Routledge & Kegan Paul, 1963).
5 Meanwhile, an unofficial stock exchange also flourishes on open ground close by, tolerated though not approved by the central authorities. Coupled with the move towards a convertible currency, the move away from licensing of industries, the lifting of tariffs on a range of imported goods and the abolition of many industrial price controls, the creation of an official stock exchange marks a fundamental shift away from a socialist command economy towards a capitalist system, albeit one with minimal political freedoms. See Ding-Xin Zhao and J. Hall, 'State Power and Patterns of Late Development', *Sociology*, vol. 28, 1994, p. 220.
6 See P. Saunders and C. Harris, *Privatization and Popular Capitalism* (Buckingham: Open University Press, 1994).
7 A. Seldon, *Capitalism* (Oxford: Basil Blackwell, 1990), p. 10.
8 In most advanced capitalist countries, of course, the existence of state welfare means that the necessity to work may be rather less compelling than it was in Marx's day – see Chapter 5.
9 'Man has almost constant occasion for the help of his brethren, and it is in vain for him to expect it from their benevolence only. He will be more likely to prevail if he can interest their self-love in his favour, and show

them that it is for their own advantage to do for him what he requires of them' (A. Smith, *The Wealth of Nations* (Harmondsworth: Pelican, 1970), p. 118).

10 'The acquisitive use of money is not exclusively modern' (Dobb, *Studies in the Development of Capitalism*, p. 8).
11 M. Weber, *Economy and Society* (New York: Bedminster Press, 1968), p. 85.
12 C. Lindblom, *Politics and Markets* (New York: Basic Books, 1977), Chapter 16.
13 Lindblom summarizes this problem in his observation that 'The human condition is small brain, big problems' (ibid., p. 66).
14 See L. von Mises, 'Economic Calculation in the Socialist Commonwealth' in F. von Hayek (ed.), *Collectivist Economic Planning* (London: Routledge, 1935); F. von Hayek, 'Socialist Calculation' in Hayek, *Individualism and Economic Order* (Chicago: University of Chicago Press, 1948).
15 Lindblom (*Politics and Markets*) cites examples from China where planned targets for coal and iron production were not met due to miscalculation of transportation requirements and where a capital construction programme failed to strike the correct balance with the production quotas for cement and timber.
16 S. Bowles and R. Edwards, *Understanding Capitalism*, 2nd edn (New York: Harper Collins, 1993).
17 Ibid.
18 B. Mitchell and H. Jones, *Second Abstract of British Historical Statistics* (Cambridge: Cambridge University Press, 1971).
19. P. Laslett, *The World We Have Lost Further Explored* (London: Methuen, 1983).
20 F. von Hayek, 'History and Politics' in Hayek, *Capitalism and the Historians* (London: Routledge & Kegan Paul, 1954).
21 F. Engels, *The Condition of the Working Class in England* (St Albans: Panther, 1969).
22 F. von Hayek, *The Constitution of Liberty* (London: Routledge & Kegan Paul, 1960).
23 P. Townsend, *Poverty in the United Kingdom* (Harmondsworth: Penguin, 1979).
24 C. Murray, *In Pursuit of Happiness and Good Government* (New York: Simon & Schuster, 1988).
25 M. Weber, *General Economic History* (New Brunswick, NJ: Transaction Books, 1981).
26 Ibid., p. 354.
27 M. Weber, *The Protestant Ethic and the Spirit of Capitalism* (London: Unwin, 1930).
28 See, for example, the essays in R. Green (ed.), *Protestantism and*

Capitalism: the Weber Thesis and its Critics (Boston: D.C. Heath, 1965); also G. Marshall, *In Search of the Spirit of Capitalism* (London: Hutchinson, 1982).

29 See Laslett, *The World We Have Lost*; P. Corrigan and D. Sayer, *The Great Arch* (Oxford: Basil Blackwell, 1985); N. Abercrombie, S. Hill and B. Turner, *The Dominant Ideology Thesis* (London: Allen & Unwin, 1980).

30 Laslett, *The World We Have Lost*.

31 Ibid.

32 C. Hill, *Reformation to Industrial Revolution* (London: Weidenfeld & Nicolson, 1967).

33 Corrigan and Sayer, *The Great Arch*.

34 Weber, *General Economic History*, pp. 342–3.

35 Corrigan and Sayer, *The Great Arch*.

36 Mann, 'European Development'.

37 Weber, *General Economic History*, Chapter 28.

38 D. Landes, 'Introduction' in Landes (ed.), *The Rise of Capitalism* (New York: Macmillan, 1966).

39 Laslett, *The World We Have Lost*.

40 Landes, 'Introduction', *The Rise of Capitalism*.

41 Mann, 'European Development'.

42 Weber, *General Economic History*, Chapter 27.

43 See Hobsbawm, *The Age of Revolution*.

44 Hobsbawm, *The Age of Capital*, p. 33.

45 The classic source of information on all this is J. Hammond and B. Hammond, *The Village Labourer* (London: Longman, 1978) which was first published in 1911. The 1978 edition also contains a useful 'General Introduction' by G. Mingay which takes issue with some of the evidence and the analysis in the original text. The discussion of the enclosures which follows is based mainly on these two sources, and on B. Moore, *Social Origins of Dictatorship and Democracy* (Harmondsworth: Allen Lane, 1967).

46 Corrigan and Sayer, *The Great Arch*.

47 Hobsbawm, *The Age of Revolution*.

Chapter 2

1 S. Bowles and R. Edwards, *Understanding Capitalism*, 2nd edn (New York: Harper Collins, 1993).

2 World Bank, *World Development Report 1993: Investing in Health* (Oxford: Oxford University Press, 1993).

3 World Bank, *World Development Report 1990: Poverty* (Oxford: Oxford University Press, 1990), p. 26.

4 World Bank, *World Development Report 1993*.

5 Mainly because they account for five-sixths of the world's industrial capacity – see World Commission on Environment and Development (the Brundtland Report), *Our Common Future* (Oxford: Oxford University Press, 1987).

6 See P. Bauer, *Equality, the Third World and Economic Delusion* (London: Methuen, 1981). Some 'underdevelopment' theorists, whose work is discussed later in this chapter, argue that capitalism is a 'world system' from which all developed countries benefit at the expense of the Third World, irrespective of particular trading links between them. Bauer's question is still pertinent, however, unless empirical research can demonstrate precisely how the wealth of a country like Switzerland has been achieved at the expense of LDCs, whether directly or indirectly.

7 This paragraph draws upon Bauer.

8 Quoted in D. Booth, 'Marxism and Development Sociology' in M. Shaw (ed.), *Marxist Sociology Revisited* (Basingstoke: Macmillan, 1985), p. 59.

9 I leave aside for the moment the question of whether the infrastructure and trading patterns established during the colonial period have locked these countries into harmful trading relations with the former imperial centres. This issue is considered separately later in this chapter.

10 Economic performance in the newly independent countries was not particularly bad relative to that of the West during the 1960s. It was only in the 1970s and 1980s that performance really began to slow down or go into reverse. See T. Killick, *Explaining Africa's Post-Independence Development Experiences* (London: Overseas Development Institute, Working Paper no. 60, 1992).

11 World Bank, *World Development Report 1993*.

12 Data are taken from E. Brett, *The World Economy since the War* (Basingstoke: Macmillan, 1985) and from World Bank, *World Development Report 1991: The Challenge of Development* (Oxford: Oxford University Press, 1991).

13 In common with many other areas of the discipline, the sociology of development was strongly influenced by Marxist theory during the 1970s, and the key figures in the field – people like Frank, Emmanuel, Wallerstein and Amin – were all writing from this perspective. For good reviews of their ideas, see D. Harrison, *The Sociology of Modernization and Development* (London: Unwin Hyman, 1988), and D. Hunt, *Economic Theories of Development* (Hemel Hempstead: Harvester Wheatsheaf, 1989).

14 See Brett, *The World Economy since the War*, Chapter 4.

15 See especially A. Emmanuel, *Unequal Exchange* (London: New Left Books, 1972).

16 See, for example, the essays in D. Booth (ed.), *Rethinking Social Development* (Harlow: Longman, 1994). In his introduction to this

volume, Booth indicates how the sociology of development has switched away from the early belief that global capitalism keeps poor countries poor, and is now more concerned to analyse the way in which internal politics affects a nation's economic performance. This switch is nowhere better exemplified than in the essay in this volume by Nicos Mouzelis, formerly one of the leading figures in underdevelopment theory. He now insists that, 'It is in fact the actual structure of the state that is the most crucial aspect for understanding why late developers with comparable starting points and resources have performed so unevenly within the world economy' ('The State in Late Development', p. 127). Understandably, perhaps, Mouzelis neglects to consider the influence of underdevelopment theory on state policies in many LDCs during the 1960s and 1970s.

17 See Ding-Xin Zhao and J. Hall, 'State Power and Patterns of Late Development', *Sociology*, vol. 28, 1994, pp. 211–20.

18 Mouzelis, 'The State in Late Development', p. 137.

19 The following discussion is based upon Hunt, *Economic Theories of Development*; Killick, *Explaining Africa's Post-Independence Development*; and J. Sender and S. Smith, *The Development of Capitalism in Africa* (London: Methuen, 1986).

20 Killick also makes the point that other, more successful, LDCs diversified out of the traditional export industries when the terms of trade turned against them, whereas countries like Zambia and Zaïre simply carried on as before. He further points out that African countries have not suffered from western protectionism as much as many other LDCs, for African exports have often been treated preferentially by the European Union and the United States, and loans have been granted at more favourable terms than was the case for, say, Latin America. All of this leads him to conclude: 'The evidence runs against those who see a hostile world economic environment as the main reason for SSA's [sub-Saharan Africa's] comparatively poor post-Independence development record' (*Explaining Africa's Post-Independence Development*, p. 21).

21 Killick (ibid.) cites an unpublished study by el-Farhan which analysed the economic performance of 32 countries in sub-Saharan Africa between 1960 and 1986. Ten possible explanatory variables -- population growth, domestic investment, government consumption, aid receipts, literacy, inflation, export growth, import growth, government debt and political stability – were entered into a multiple regression model. The strongest effect was found to be export performance. Domestic investment and political stability were also found to be significant, while the other factors were not. When changes in the commodity terms of trade were entered into the model, this variable too feel short of statistical significance.

22 This is one aspect of the colonial legacy which could be said to have held

back development in LDCs, for in Africa in particular, national boundaries are based upon the former colonial territories which cut across traditional ethnic and tribal divisions. The resulting civil strife and political instability since independence has been a significant factor in crippling many of these economies.

23 It is remarkable to recall, for example, that as recently as 1970, Taiwan's per capita GDP was lower than that of Sudan (see *The Sunday Times*, 15 May 1994).

24 World Bank, *World Development Report 1991*.

25 Cited in D. Evans, 'Visible and Invisible Hands in Trade Policy Reform' in C. Colclough and J. Manor (eds), *States or Markets?* (Oxford: Clarendon Press, 1993).

26 See P. Berger, *The Capitalist Revolution* (Aldershot: Wildwood House, 1987) from which the data on the other 'little dragons' have also been taken. See also M. Friedman and R. Friedman, *Free to Choose* (London: Secker & Warburg, 1980).

27 G. Taber, 'Growing, Growing', *Time International*, vol. 140, no. 11, 14 September 1992, pp. 20–4.

28 World Bank, *The East Asian Miracle* (Oxford: Oxford University Press, 1993).

29 Zhao and Hall, 'State Power'; F. Fukuyama, 'The End of History?', *The National Interest*, Summer 1989, pp. 1–18.

30 Berger, *The Capitalist Revolution*.

31 World Bank, *The East Asian Miracle*.

32 Ibid.

33 In fact, in most cases development has brought greater equalization of incomes in its wake without any need for redistributive policies by government. Berger (*The Capitalist Revolution*) shows that, in Japan, the early period of industrialization increased income inequalities which then flattened out later to a point where inequality became *less* marked than in countries such as Britain and Sweden which pursued explicit policies of redistribution until quite recently. In South Korea and Taiwan, income distribution became more equal right from the start of the industrialization process.

34 There have been some exceptions to this. In the 1950s, for example, the Ministry of International Trade and Industry in Japan tried (unsuccessfully) to steer new investment into steel, chemicals and ship-building while at the same time advising Sony against developing transistors and warning Honda to keep out of car production! (see W. Kasper, 'Firing Up the Little Dragons', *Economic Affairs*, vol. 11, 1990, pp. 21–2). Since then, however, both Japan and the smaller east Asian governments have followed market signals rather than trying to lead them.

35 Data from *The Sunday Times*, 13 March 1994.

Chapter 3

1 Not all greens are critical of capitalism, for as we shall see later, some believe that the market mechanism and private property rights can be used to solve environmental problems. In this chapter I shall draw an admittedly crude distinction between 'deep greens', who seek solutions through deindustrialization and a transcendence of capitalism, and 'green capitalists', who seek solutions within existing social, economic and political frameworks.

2 J. Porritt and D. Winner, *The Coming of the Greens* (London: Fontana, 1988), p. 233.

3 World Commission on Environment and Development (the Brundtland Report), *Our Common Future* (Oxford: Oxford University Press, 1987).

4 See L. Martell, *Ecology and Society* (Cambridge: Polity Press, 1994), p. 44.

5 Porritt and Winner, *The Coming of the Greens*.

6 D. Pearce, E. Barber, A. Markandya, S. Barrett, R. Turner and T. Swanson, *Blueprint 2: Greening the World Economy* (London: Earthscan Publications, 1991).

7 Martell, *Ecology*, p. 49.

8 Quoted in D. Ray, *Trashing the Planet* (Washington, DC: Regnery Gateway, 1990), p. 169.

9 See Martell, *Ecology*, p. 27; also *The Sunday Times*, 17 July 1994.

10 Pearce et al., *Blueprint 2*. These figures are very rough estimates and are widely contested. It is, however, also worth noting the estimate from the same source that 35 per cent of this forest clearance since 1980 can be seen as a response to incentives (tax breaks, farm subsidies, export subsidies) offered to farmers by the Brazilian government. The problem of the rainforest has been caused as much by governments as by global markets.

11 United Nations Environment Programme, *Environmental Data Report 1993–94* (Oxford: Basil Blackwell, 1994); R. Whelan, *Mounting Greenery* (London: Institute of Economic Affairs, 1989).

12 The link between sulphur emissions, acid rain, and the death of forests has, however, never been demonstrated, and there is now an increasing view among scientists that the problem in the Black Forest may have more to do with increasing levels of ozone than with acidity in the rainfall.

13 New Economics Foundation, *Measuring Sustainable Economic Welfare* (London: New Economics Foundation, 1994).

14 *The Sunday Times*, 27 March 1994.

15 See Ray, *Trashing the Planet*, for a comprehensive review of the evidence.

16 R. Bate and J. Morris, *Global Warming: Apocalypse or Hot Air?* (London: Institute of Economic Affairs, 1994).

17 R. Balling, 'Interpreting the Global Temperature Record', *Economic Affairs*, vol. 14, 1994, pp. 18–21. See also Ray, *Trashing the Planet*.

18 Report in *The Independent*, 25 July 1994.

19 Ray, *Trashing the Planet*; Bate and Morris, *Global Warming*; also the debate in *Nature*, 27 January 1994.

20 See Ray, *Trashing the Planet*. On 7 April 1994, *The Independent* reported that research on meteorological records in Northern Ireland dating back to 1795 had found a strong correlation between air temperatures and rates of solar activity.

21 R. Lewis 'Global Hysteria', *Economic Affairs*, vol. 11, 1991, pp. 4–6.

22 Ray, *Trashing the Planet*.

23 This could support the theory that, as with global warming, the cause of fluctuations in the ozone layer is to be found in sunspot activity – see Lewis, 'Global Hysteria'.

24 Ray, *Trashing the Planet*.

25 Ibid.

26 Ibid.

27 The estimate is made by Lewis, 'Global Hysteria'.

28 D. Pearce, A. Markandya and E. Barbier, *Blueprint for a Green Economy* (London: Earthscan Publications, 1989).

29 A case in point is the huge investment currently going into meeting European Union water quality standards, for the marginal cost of removing the last minute traces of nitrates or iron from the drinking water supply almost certainly exceeds any marginal benefit that might accrue in terms of reductions in possible health risks – see M. Carney, 'The Cost of Compliance with Ever Higher Quality Standards' in T. Gilland (ed.), *The Changing Water Business* (London: Centre for the Study of the Regulated Industries, 1992).

30 Whelan, *Mounting Greenery*.

31 'Obviously, capitalism creates more value and greater resources than it consumes. That is why it creates wealth' (K. Jeffreys, 'Free Market Environmentalism: Can It Save the Planet?', *Economic Affairs*, vol. 14, 1994, p. 9). As Jeffreys points out, the objective of bequeathing to the future at least as much as we ourselves inherited from the past can only mean, either, leaving everything untouched, or exploiting resources in order to create more wealth than was around before. Similarly, Whelan concludes that 'The best way to provide for future generations is to exploit resources, not conserve them' (*Mounting Greenery*, p. 29).

32 Whelan, *Mounting Greenery*.

33 See Martell, *Ecology*, pp. 72–75 for an outline of this argument.

34 Cited in ibid., p. 74.

35 Even seemingly huge and intractable problems such as global warming may have technical solutions. Not only is research continuing into non-carbon-based sources of energy such as wind farms, but it may also

be possible to reduce current levels of carbon dioxide in the atmosphere through, for example, seeding the oceans with iron in order to stimulate the growth of algae which absorb CO_2 and take it to the seabed when they die.

36 In an otherwise sympathetic discussion of radical green ideas, Martell (*Ecology*) develops an unanswerable critique of those who believe that green objectives can be met through a move to decentralized, voluntary and largely self-sufficient communities. The basic problem is that, without a centralized, coordinating power, there will be nothing to oblige each community to follow green practice. This means that the use of centralized power is an unavoidable condition of effective green politics – but this then raises the spectre of state coercion used as an instrument against all those who do not come into line with the new austerity programme. This dilemma is, of course, already familiar from more than a century of socialist writing where futile attempts have been made to reconcile the desire for revolutionary social change with the desire to avoid totalitarian forms of politics – see P. Saunders 'When Prophecy Fails', *Economy and Society*, vol. 22, 1993, pp. 89–99.

37 G. Hardin, 'The Tragedy of the Commons' in G. Hardin and J. Baden (eds), *Managing the Commons* (San Francisco: W.H. Freeman, 1977), p. 20.

38 Though as we shall see, not all green thinkers draw this conclusion.

39 Brundtland Report, p. 1.

40 Porritt and Winner, *The Coming of the Greens*, pp. 263 and 11.

41 A. Dobson, *Green Political Thought* (London: Harper Collins, 1990), pp. 175 and 178. Similarly, Martell (*Ecology*) is in no doubt that greens share with socialists a commitment to the overthrow of capitalism, and he urges the green movement to form alliances with socialist parties (p. 13).

42 The Russian Environment Minister suggested at the end of 1993 that about 15 per cent of the country should be considered an environmental disaster zone. Half of all arable land was unsuitable for farming, four-fifths of industrial waste was inadequately treated, hundreds of rivers were polluted with nuclear waste, and 100,000 people were living on land which was dangerously irradiated (*The Independent*, 28 December 1993).

43 T. Anderson and D. Leal, *Free Market Environmentalism* (Boulder, CO: Westview Press, 1991). I. Sugg and U. Kreuter, *Elephants and Ivory* (London: Institute of Economic Affairs, 1994).

44 M. Sas-Rolfes, 'Trade in Endangered Species', *Economic Affairs*, vol. 14, 1994, pp. 10–12.

45 Martell, *Ecology*.

46 Saunders and Harris, *Privatization*, Chapter 5.

47 *Independent on Sunday*, 2 January 1994.

48 Anderson and Leal, *Free Market Environmentalism*.

49 Ibid.
50 Pearce *et al.*, *Blueprint 2*.

Chapter 4

1 A. Maslow, 'A Theory of Human Motivation', *Psychological Review*, vol. 50, 1943, pp. 371–96.
2 C. Murray, *In Pursuit of Happiness and Good Government* (New York: Simon & Schuster, 1988).
3 K. Marx, *The Economic and Philosophic Manuscripts of 1844* (New York: International Publishers, 1964), p. 114.
4 Ibid., p. 111.
5 H. Marcuse, *One Dimensional Man* (London: Routledge & Kegan Paul, 1964).
6 F. Hirsch, *Social Limits to Growth* (Cambridge, MA: Harvard University Press, 1976), pp. 6–7.
7 E. Durkheim, *Suicide* (London: Routledge & Kegan Paul, 1952), p. 248.
8 C. Campbell, *The Romantic Ethic and the Spirit of Modern Consumerism* (Oxford: Basil Blackwell, 1987).
9 F. Tönnies, *Community and Society* (New York: Harper & Row, 1955), p. 3.
10 Central Statistical Office (CSO), *Social Trends* (London: HMSO, 1994).
11 Reported in R. Lane, *The Market Experience* (Cambridge: Cambridge University Press, 1991), p. 507.
12 A. Giddens, 'A Reply to My Critics' in D. Held and J. Thompson, (eds), *Social Theory of Modern Societies* (Cambridge: Cambridge University Press, 1989).
13 See G. Simmel, 'The Metropolis and Mental Life' in K. Wolff (ed.), *The Sociology of Georg Simmel* (Glencoe, Il: Free Press, 1950).
14 R. Wall, 'The Household: Demographic and Economic Change in England, 1650–1970' in R. Wall (ed.), *Family Forms in Historic Europe* (Cambridge: Cambridge University Press, 1983).
15 C. Fischer, *Networks and Places* (New York: Free Press, 1977).
16 See the discussion of work by Gans, Pahl and others in P. Saunders, *Social Theory and the Urban Question*, 2nd edn (London: Hutchinson, 1986).
17 CSO, *Social Trends*, 1994.
18 C. Murray, *Underclass: The Crisis Deepens* (London: Institute of Economic Affairs, 1994).
19 CSO, *Social Trends*, 1994.
20 N. Dennis and G. Erdos, *Families without Fatherhood*, 2nd edn (London: Institute of Economic Affairs, 1993).

21 C. Mirrlees-Black and N. Maung, *Fear of Crime* (London: Home Office Research & Statistics Department, 1994).

22 CSO, *Social Trends*, 1994.

23 Department of Employment, *Family Expenditure Survey* (London: HMSO, 1994).

24 See R. Merton, 'Social Structure and Anomie', in Merton, *Social Theory and Social Structure* (New York: Free Press, 1957).

25 For example, D. Green, *Reinventing Civil Society* (London: Institute of Economic Affairs, 1993).

26 Dennis and Erdos, *Families*.

27 C. Murray, *The Emerging British Underclass* (London: Institute of Economic Affairs, 1990).

28 Examples are given in Murray, *Underclass: The Crisis Deepens*.

29 For an analysis of the link between crime and the erosion of the culture of individual responsibility, see J. Wilson, 'Incivility and Crime' in E. Banfield (ed.), *Civility and Citizenship*, (New York: Paragon House, 1992).

30 N. Abercrombie, S. Hill and B. Turner, *Sovereign Individuals of Capitalism* (London: Allen & Unwin, 1986), p. 1.

31 Green, *Reinventing Civil Society*.

32 The phrase was originally coined by Edmund Burke but is taken up by Murray, *In Pursuit of Happiness*. See also P. Berger and R. Neuhaus, *To Empower People* (Washington, DC: American Enterprise Institute for Public Policy Research, 1977).

33 I have developed this argument further in P. Saunders, 'Citizenship in a Liberal Society' in B. Turner (ed.), *'Citizenship and Social Theory* (London: Sage, 1993). Interestingly, Abercrombie, Hill and Turner develop a comparable argument when they suggest that it was the 'struggle for citizenship rights against capitalism' which led to modern forms of individuation (*Sovereign Individuals*, p. 154).

34 R. Blauner, *Alienation and Freedom* (Chicago: University of Chicago Press, 1964).

35 See, for example, S. Clegg, *Modern Organisations* (London: Sage, 1990).

36 Department of Employment and Productivity, *British Labour Statistics Historical Abstract 1886–1968* (London: HMSO, 1971); CSO, *Social Trends*, 1994. In the United States, the proportion of the workforce employed in manufacturing fell from 27 per cent to 17 per cent between 1970 and 1990 (OECD, *Labour Force Statistics* (Paris: OECD), 1992).

37 Murray, *In Pursuit of Happiness*.

38 See, for example, J. Klein, *Samples from English Cultures* (London: Routledge & Kegan Paul, 1965).

39 For the contrasting argument, see R. Sennett and J. Cobb, *The Hidden Injuries of Class* (Cambridge: Cambridge University Press, 1972).

40 J. Goldthorpe with C. Llewellyn and C. Payne, *Social Mobility and Class Structure in Modern Britain*, 2nd edn, (Oxford: Clarendon Press, 1987).

41 P. Saunders, 'Could Britain be a Meritocracy?', *Sociology*, vol. 29, forthcoming, 1995.

42 Lane, *The Market Experience*, p. 235.

43 Ibid., p. 154.

44 H. Stretton, *Urban Planning in Rich and Poor Countries* (Oxford: Oxford University Press, 1978).

45 J. Gershuny, *After Industrial Society?* (London: Macmillan, 1978).

46 R. Pahl, *Divisions of Labour* (Oxford: Basil Blackwell, 1984), p. 105.

47 Stretton, *Urban Planning*, p. 54.

Chapter 5

1 The Sunday Times, *Britain's Richest 500* (London: The Sunday Times, 1994).

2 One example is the persistent attempt by the European Union to protect its agriculture and industry from cheaper competition from the Third World and to fix exchange rates in the face of world currency markets.

3 F. Fukuyama, 'The End of History?', *The National Interest*, Summer 1989, p. 4. See also his further development of these ideas in F. Fukuyama, *The End of History and the Last Man* (London: Penguin, 1992).

4 Fukuyama, 'The End of History?', p. 18.

5 M. Weber, 'Politics as a Vocation' in H. Gerth and C. Wright Mills (eds), *From Max Weber* (London: Routledge & Kegan Paul, 1948).

6 Capitalism can flourish under both liberal and totalitarian political regimes, although a free economy is probably a condition of a free polity – see M. Friedman, *Capitalism and Freedom* (Chicago: University of Chicago Press, 1962). Fukuyama makes the same error as Marx in assuming a necessary causal link between the 'economic base' of a society and its 'political superstructure'. For an extended analysis of this issue in Marxist theory, see B. Jessop, 'Capitalism and Democracy: the Best Possible Political Shell?' in G. Littlejohn (ed.), *Power and the State* (London: Croom Helm, 1978).

7 M. Albert, *Capitalism against Capitalism* (London: Whurr Publishers, 1993).

8 Ibid., pp. 18–19.

9 Ibid., p. 53.

10 Ibid., p. 79.

11 Many of these policies have been extended to the whole of the

European Union where Britain alone continues to resist them (e.g. through its opt-out from the Social Chapter of the Maastricht Treaty).

12 Albert, *Capitalism against Capitalism*, p. 204.

13 E. Durkheim, *The Division of Labor in Society* (Toronto: Macmillan, 1933).

14 R. Dore, *British Factory, Japanese Factory* (London: George Allen & Unwin, 1973), p. 209.

15 Ibid., p. 215.

16 For examples of such 'interference', see R. Huntford, *The New Totalitarians* (London: Allen Lane, 1971).

17 Quoted in R. Segalman and D. Marsland, *Cradle to Grave* (Basingstoke: Macmillan, 1989), p. 92.

18 See N. Abercrombie, S. Hill and B. Turner, *Sovereign Individuals of Capitalism* (London: Allen & Unwin, 1986).

19 J. Schumpeter, *Capitalism, Socialism and Democracy* (London: George Allen & Unwin, 1943), p. 142.

20 N. Dennis, *Rising Crime and the Dismembered Family* (London: Institute of Economic Affairs, 1993).

21 D. Bell, *The Cultural Contradictions of Capitalism* (London: Heinemann, 1976).

22 G. Himmelfarb, *The Demoralization of Society* (New York: Knopps, 1995).

23 See, for example, J. Lyotard, *The Postmodern Condition* (Manchester: Manchester University Press, 1984); S. Lash and J. Urry, *The End of Organized Capitalism* (Cambridge: Polity Press, 1987).

24 There is a central dilemma within liberalism that toleration leads eventually to its own destruction since it has no way of repressing intolerable practices – see S. Mendus, *Toleration and the Limits of Liberalism* (Basingstoke: Macmillan, 1989).

25 'The moralities which protect every individual from being harmed by others, either directly or by being hindered in his freedom of pursuing his own good, are at once those which he himself has most at heart, and those which he has the strongest interest in publishing and enforcing by word and deed' (J.S. Mill, 'Utilitarianism' in J. Gray (ed.), *John Stuart Mill on Liberty and Other Essays* (Oxford. Oxford University Press, 1991, p. 196)).

26 See, for example, M. Novak, *The Spirit of Democratic Capitalism* (New York: Simon & Schuster, 1982), or the essays in J. Davies (ed.), *God and the Marketplace* (London: Institute of Economic Affairs, 1993). Interestingly, self-styled 'ethical socialists' like Norman Dennis and Chelly Halsey share with these writers a concern about the erosion of a public morality – see N. Dennis and G. Erdos *Families without Fatherhood*, 2nd edn (London: Institute of Economic Affairs, 1993).

Index

Abercrombie, N., 93
absolutism, 19–20
acid rain, 54, 58, 63, 74–5, 127
advertising, 6, 79
Africa, 30, 32, 34, 36, 41, 42–4, 48, 61, 125
agriculture, 18–19, 23, 26–7, 34, 48, 58
  see also enclosures, food supplies
Albert, M., 107–12, 115, 116
alienation, 78–80, 95, 101
  see also self-actualization
anomie, 82, 113
aristocracy, 18–19, 49
Australia, 33, 34, 74, 113

Bell, D., 117, 118
Berger, P., 48
Blauner, R., 95
body, private rights over, 4
Body Shop, 71
bourgeoisie, 19
  see also capitalist class
bourgeois culture
  erosion of, 16–17, 92, 109, 116–20
  in east Asia, 48–9
  see also work ethic
Brazil, 42, 46, 51
  rainforest, 57–8, 127

Brundtland Report, 53–4, 55–6, 64, 68

California Clean Air Incentives Market, 73
Campbell, C., 82
Canada, 33
capital, ownership of, 103
capitalist class
  alliance with landowners, 19
  decline of, 103, 117
  role of, 78
Caribbean, 30, 36
charity, 93–4, 116
China, 4, 9, 15, 36, 41–2, 46, 48, 56, 104, 106, 121
church, 86
  see also religion
cities, 10, 18–20
  see also urbanization
citizenship rights, 92, 94, 112, 119
city states, 19
Civil War in England, 18–19
class system, 96
  see also social mobility
Club of Rome Report, 57
collectivism, 49, 93, 108, 110, 113–15
colonialism, 5, 21, 27, 31, 32–4, 39, 47, 125–6

commercial capitalism, 1–2, 27
  see also merchants
communications, 10, 15, 39, 87
community, 78, 83–8
competition, 8, 9, 10, 80, 97, 102,
    111, 116
  spur to efficiency, 42, 50
competitive advantage, 40, 45, 50
Confucianism, 93
conscription, 5, 113
consumerism, 69, 79–83, 117
  green consumerism, 70–1
consumer sovereignty, 9, 99
corporate capitalism, 6, 82, 103,
    107, 111, 115, 116, 117
  see also transnational corpor-
    ations
corruption, 8, 44, 109
credit, 7, 21, 109, 117
crime, 89–93, 114
crises in capitalism, 8, 102–3

Dennis, N., 89, 91
definition of capitalism, 9
deindustrialization, 54
  see also manufacturing, decline
    of
dependency theory, 36–8
  see also underdevelopment
    theories
divorce, 88, 91
domestic self-provisioning, *see*
    self-service economy
Dore, R., 114
Durkheim, E., 81–2, 113

east Asia, 27, 33, 36, 40, 45–51
  see also under specific countries
economic growth
  created by capitalism, 9–12
  critique of, 52, 76, 81
  international comparisons, 35–6,
    43, 46, 47
  limits to, 53–5

enclosures, 13, 25–7, 49, 67, 85
energy supplies, 30, 52, 54, 64–5
Engels, F., 13
England
  break-up of feudalism, 2
  kinship system, 87
  origins of capitalism in, 15, 18–27
  population growth, 11
  spread of capitalism from, 10
  see also Great Britain
environment, 52–76
  changed by human intervention,
    53
  commodification of, 69–76
  costs of environmental
    regulation, 62–5
  pricing the environment, 63
  technological solutions to
    problems, 65–7
Erdos, G., 89, 91
Ethiopia, 33, 43
etymology of 'capitalism', 1
European Union, 104, 132
export-oriented growth, 38, 40,
    45–51

factory system, 22–3, 24, 95
family
  breakdown of, 88–9
  change with industrialization, 87
  patriarchy, 116
  single parents, 88–9, 91, 92, 115
  source of social unity, 84
  surveillance by, 86
fascism, 105–6
feudalism
  compared with capitalism, 4, 8
  in Europe, 2, 82
finance markets, 2, 8, 18
  difference between neo-
    American and Rhine models,
    108, 109–10, 111
  ethical investment, 71
financial institutions, 103, 110

Fischer, C., 87
Florence, 2, 15, 18, 21
food supplies, 27, 35, 48, 55
France, 4, 18, 19, 22
freedom, personal, 86, 88, 112, 119
free markets, 7–9, 47
  condition of political freedom, 132
free rider problem, 68
Freud, S., 79
Fukuyama, F., 105, 120

gentry, 18, 19, 22
Germany, 73, 104, 109, 112, 113
  economic culture, 82, 108, 110–11
  growth of capitalism, 18, 22, 24, 27, 49
  see also Rhine model capitalism
Ghana, 43–4
globalization of capitalism, 2–3, 10, 37, 104, 105, 111
global warming, 54, 55, 59–61, 71, 73
Goldthorpe, J., 97–8
government, *see* State
Great Britain
  crime rates, 89, 91
  culture, 112–13
  economic growth, 11, 33, 46
  family change, 88–9
  labour force, 95
  opportunities, 97–8
  unemployment, 85
  welfare state, 91, 108
  see also England
Great Exhibition, 1, 54
green critique of capitalism, 52–5, 66, 67–9
green movement
  affinity with socialism, 67, 68–9, 107, 129
  changing concerns of, 55, 62

draconian prescriptions, 56–7, 69, 75
  popularity of, 54, 107
growth, *see* economic growth
guild system, 2, 8, 21–2

happiness
  conditions of, 77–8, 101
  sources of dissatisfaction, 80–3, 118
Hardin, G., 68
Hayek, F., 9, 14
Hirsch, F., 81
history, end of, 103–7, 120
Hong Kong, 33, 46, 47, 49

ideology, 105–7
immigration, 104, 112
immiseration thesis, 12–15, 30, 78
import substitution, 42, 46, 51
  see also protectionism
India, 15, 29, 30, 32, 33, 34, 36, 41, 51, 61
individualism, 15, 49, 84, 86, 90, 93–4, 109, 113, 114, 115, 116, 117–19
Indonesia, 48, 49, 50
industrial capitalism, spread of, 2
  see also technology
industrial revolution, 10, 13, 64, 87
inequality, 13, 30, 36, 90, 108, 109, 126
infant mortality, 12, 30, 109
innovation, 8, 10–11, 52, 66, 114
  see also technology
interest, *see* finance markets, usury
intelligentsia, 116
intimacy, *see* community
Islam, 106
Italy, 2, 15, 18, 19, 21
Ivory Coast, 43, 44

Japan, 33, 50, 104, 106, 109, 112,
113
  economic culture, 82, 93, 108,
  110–11, 113–14
  economic growth, 11, 27, 29, 40,
  46, 48, 49–50
Jevons, S., 64

Kenya, 43, 70
Keynesianism, 104
Killick, T., 43

labour process, *see* work
land market, 2, 8
land reform, 42, 49, 50
Lane, R., 99–101
Laslett, P., 13
Latin America, 30, 36, 41, 42, 48
  see also Brazil
law, 18, 20, 27, 34, 44, 49, 82, 91,
  93, 115
legitimacy, 117, 118, 119
less developed countries, *see* third
  world
liberalism, 105–6, 107, 113, 114,
  117, 118, 120, 133
life expectancy, 12, 30, 35, 53
Lloyd, W., 67
London, before industrial
  revolution, 19
Low Countries, *see* Netherlands

Magna Carta, 19, 20
malady of infinite aspiration, 81
Malaysia, 34, 46, 48
managerialism, 116
Manchester, growth of, 26
manufacturing, decline of, 95, 104,
  108
Marcuse, H., 79–80
markets
  determine prices, 7–9
  morality of, 119

relation to liberal democracy,
  107
social functions, 90, 94, 100
see also supply and demand
Marx, K., 1, 4, 6, 12, 13, 30, 78–9,
  94, 101, 102, 106
Maslow, A., 77–8, 85
mass society, 79, 117
materialism, 79
  see also consumerism
mercantilism, 21
  see also commercial capitalism
merchants, 2, 18, 21–2
meritocracy, 14, 97–8
Microsoft, 103
Mill, J.S., 119
Mises, L., 9
modernity, 1, 54–5, 86, 87, 117, 120
monarchy, 19–20
money
  dehumanizes social relations, 84,
  86
  system of exchange, 2, 7
monopoly, 103, 111
morality, 81, 90, 109, 114, 115,
  117–20
Murray, C., 78, 88, 96, 99

nationalism, 106
nationalized industries, 4, 44
natural resources, 57–8, 62, 64, 70
  see also energy supplies, food
  supplies
needs
  false, 79–80
  hierarchy of, 78–9
  not met under capitalism, 5–6, 99
neo-American capitalism, 6, 49,
  107–11, 112, 113, 115, 116
Netherlands, 2, 15, 18, 20, 21,
  108

occupational system, 95–7
open parish system, 22, 25

origins of capitalism, 1–2, 93
    see also pre-conditions of
        capitalist development
ozone layer, 55, 59, 61–2

Pahl, R., 101
peasantry, 26, 38
planning, 102, 104, 115
pollution, 55, 58–9, 65, 68, 72
    charges and taxes, 72–5
popular culture, 79, 112, 117
population growth, 11–12, 15, 19,
        27, 55
    as a problem, 52, 55–7
Portugal, 15
positional goods, 80–1
postmodernism, 66, 118–19
poverty
    definitions of, 14, 29
    in USA, 109
    in early capitalism, 13
    in third world, 29–32
preconditions of capitalist
        development, 15–18
prices
    controls over, 7, 8, 21, 42, 50
    environmental pricing, 63, 72–5
    information system, 9, 65
privatization, 4, 51, 74–5
production
    as means to an end, 5, 16
    planned, 8–9
    see also planning
profit, 5–7, 9
    ignores the general good, 58–9
    harnessed for the general good,
        70–4, 119
    tendency to fall, 102
property rights, 3–5, 9, 18, 70,
        73–4, 116
protectionism, 41–4, 46
    see also tariffs, trade
Protestantism, 15–17, 49, 82–3, 117
    see also religion, work ethic

putting out system, 2, 22–3, 25, 27

quality of life, 77, 88
    see also happiness

racism, 104–5, 112
rationality, 6, 15, 16, 84, 107, 116,
        117, 119
recession, 103
    see also crises in capitalism
relativism, 117, 118, 119
religion, 15–17, 21, 48–9, 82, 84,
        93, 109, 116
    see also under specific religions
revolution, 18, 67, 103
Rhine model capitalism, 82, 108,
        110–15
risk, 6, 7–8, 66–7, 85
romanticism, 12–13, 83, 115
Rowntree, S., 14
rule of law, 20
    see also law
ruling class, 19
rural way of life, 12–13, 87–8
Russia, 4, 69, 90
    see also Soviet Union

safety, *see* security
saving, 109, 116
Schumpeter, J., 116–17, 118
security, 78, 83, 85, 89–90
    ontological, 85
self-actualization, 78, 94, 99–101
    see also alienation
self-esteem, 78, 95–8
self-help, 93–4
self-interest, 5, 68, 76, 84, 93, 109,
        119
    see also individualism
self-service economy, 100–1
service class, 97, 117
share ownership, 103, 110
    see also corporate capitalism,
        financial institutions

Simmel, G., 86
Singapore, 46, 48, 49, 50
slavery
    cause of third world poverty, 31,
        32
    compared with capitalism, 4
Smith, A., 5
socialism
    compared with capitalism, 3–4,
        5, 8,
    environmental catastrophes
        under, 69, 129
    failure of, 8–9, 104
    third world, 41–4, 46
social mobility, 14, 97–8
South Korea, 33, 46, 48, 49, 50
Soviet Union, 3, 9, 34, 104, 106
    see also Russia
Spain, 15
standard of living
    newly industrialized countries,
        48
    past and present, 11, 13–14
    poor and rich countries, 29–30,
        35, 54
State
    fragmented power, 20
    government failure, 70
    intervention in capitalism, 4, 7,
        48–51, 67, 71–6, 92, 94, 104,
        110–11, 126
    relation to civil society, 113
    third world, 42, 125
status, 96–7
Stretton, H., 101
supply and demand, 7, 65
sustainable development, 55–6, 64,
        128
Sweden, 33, 114–15
Switzerland, 31, 33, 108, 112, 113,
        115

Taiwan, 33, 48, 49, 50
Tanzania, 43, 44, 47, 51

tariffs, 7, 42, 45, 47, 49, 111
    see also protectionism
technology, 9, 10–11, 18, 23–4, 27,
        39, 40, 46, 64, 65–7, 74, 80, 102
    critique of, 52, 54, 65–6
    impact on work, 94–5, 99
Thackeray, W., 1
Thailand, 46, 48, 50
Thatcher, M., 90–1, 117
third world
    cost of environmental policies,
        62, 63–4
    economic development, 35–45,
        54
    government policies, 42–4, 49,
        125
    growth of capitalism in, 10, 51
    population growth, 35, 55
    poverty, 29–30
    relationship with western
        countries, 31–2, 36–41, 125
Tönnies, F., 84, 86, 89, 93
Townsend, P., 14
trade
    expansion of, 1–2, 21, 23, 24, 84
    free, 7, 18, 47, 110
    government control of, 8, 20–2,
        43–4
    ivory, 70
    slave, 32
    terms of, 43, 125
    see also protectionism, unequal
        exchange
trade unions, 111
tragedy of the commons, 67–8, 69,
        70
transnational corporations, 31,
        37–8
transport, 10, 24, 75, 87

Uganda, 43, 44
unemployment, 85, 90, 104
underdevelopment theories, 36–41
    see also depedency theory

unequal exchange, 38–41, 125
urbanization, 85
    see also cities
urban way of life, 87
USA, 6, 8, 29, 32, 104, 107–10
    crime rates, 89, 109
    culture, 112–13
    economic decline, 108–10
    economic growth, 11, 46
    growth of capitalism, 10, 24, 27
    unemployment, 85
    welfare, 91–2, 108
    see also neo-American capitalism
usury, 8
    see also finance markets

wage controls, 8, 42, 50
wage labour, 1, 7, 8, 18, 19, 24–6
Warren, B., 34
wealth, 'trickle-down', 13–14
Weber, M., 6, 15–18, 20, 23, 82–3,
    106
welfare provision, 4, 47, 49, 50, 85,
    90, 104, 118
    difference between neo-
        American and Rhine models,
        108, 110, 114–15

erodes individual responsibility,
    91–2, 118
Whelan, R., 58
women, 92, 96, 118
World Bank, 29, 35, 46
work
    instrumental orientation to, 79,
        118
    organization of, 94–7, 99–100
    reduced need for, 100
work ethic, 16, 22, 48–9, 83, 92,
    109, 116, 117
    see also bourgeois culture
working class
    condition of, 13–14, 78, 111
    creation of, 26, 103
    decline of, 95
    opportunities, 97–8
    traditional way of life, 96, 117

yuppies, 90

Zaïre, 29, 43
Zambia, 39, 47, 51
Zimbabwe, 70